The Don's Brother Method

The Don's Brother Method

HOW I THRU-HIKED THE APPALACHIAN TRAIL AND RARELY SLEPT IN THE WOODS

Mike Stephens

Copyright © 2016 Mike Stephens
All rights reserved.

ISBN-13: 9781530473014
ISBN-10: 1530473012
Library of Congress Control Number: 2016904365
CreateSpace Independent Publishing Platform
North Charleston, South Carolina

Dedication

*Again for family:
Linda, Rachel, and Lisa
Sam, Amanda, Case, and Copelan
Brent, Lori, and Macy*

And in Memory Of:

*My parents, Johnnie and Elizabeth
And my brother, Don*

Acknowledgements

AS WITH MY FIRST BOOK, *Don's Brother: A Hike of Hope on the Appalachian Trail*, I wish to thank my wife, Linda, for her support during the planning stages of my hike, while I was on the trail, and as I have been working on this second book.

I feel enormously blessed by all of my family. My son, Sam, my daughter, Rachel, and my nephew, and Don's son, Brent, inspired me throughout the hike and continued to be an inspiration as I worked on *The Don's Brother Method*.

I would like to thank my good friends Kay Agnew, Beth Parr, and Renea Woodard, and my wife, Linda, for taking the time to proofread my material before I submitted it for publication.

I would also like to thank Jenny Horton who designed the cover for *The Don's Brother Method*. In addition, I would like to give cover photo credits to Mike Culpepper and Laura Parker Gray.

My hike may not have been accomplished without all the wonderful people I met along my way. For those who offered a ride to or from the trail, to those who shared a meal with me, to the many who just sent me a message or offered up a prayer, I am eternally grateful.

I hiked with dozens of thru-hikers, section-hikers, and day-hikers from Georgia to Maine. There is no way to list them all, but each contributed in a special way to my journey.

I would especially like to thank John "Molar Man" Eichelberger and his wife, Diane, "Sweet Tooth" for their friendship and support. I would also like to thank sincerely my other hiking companions, Joe "Pilgrim" Estes, Doug "Banzai" Douma, Walt "Susquehanna Slim" Krzastek, and Renea "Speck" Woodard. Each of you played an important role in the success of the Don's Brother Method.

I would also like to acknowledge David "Awol" Miller whose invaluable resource, *The A.T. Guide*, I used throughout my hike. Were it not for this book, the Don's Brother Method of hiking the Appalachian Trail would have been much more challenging. Even though my thru-hike was in 2013, I used the 2012 edition. The A.T. changes slightly every year, so it's a good idea to have the most recent version of Awol's book.

And finally, I would like to thank God for giving me the strength, courage, and ability to accomplish my task. Every day I felt His presence and earnestly feel that He placed every one of the people that I met on the trail in my life for a reason.

Table of Contents

Acknowledgements ·vii
Introduction · xiii

Chapter 1   But I Don't Want to Sleep in the Woods! · · · · · · · · · · · · · · · · 1
Chapter 2   Places to Sleep in Georgia · 6
Chapter 3   A Shelter Here; A Hostel There ·12
Chapter 4   Over 300 Miles of Beds and Bunks · · · · · · · · · · · · · · · · ·18
Chapter 5   Avoiding the Virginia Blues ·32
Chapter 6   Shenandoah Snoozing · 42
Chapter 7   Maryland and Molar Man ·51
Chapter 8   The Light Pack Prevails in Pennsylvania · · · · · · · · · · · · · ·55
Chapter 9   Rocks and Rooms in Northern PA · · · · · · · · · · · · · · · · ·61
Chapter 10 Roads and Delis in New Jersey and New York · · · · · · · · · · · ·65
Chapter 11 Towns in Connecticut ·73
Chapter 12 Motels of Massachusetts · 80
Chapter 13 Vermont Lodging ·91
Chapter 14 The Huts of New Hampshire and Some Motels As Well · · · · 101
Chapter 15 Sleeping Snuggly in Rugged Maine · · · · · · · · · · · · · · · · ·121
Chapter 16 Slackpacking the Wilderness ·140
Chapter 17 Another Bed in Bangor ·157
Chapter 18 A Hike Without a Tent ·159
Chapter 19 Fine-Tuning the DBM ·161
Chapter 20 Hike Your Own Hike ·168

Appendix ·173
About the Author ·181

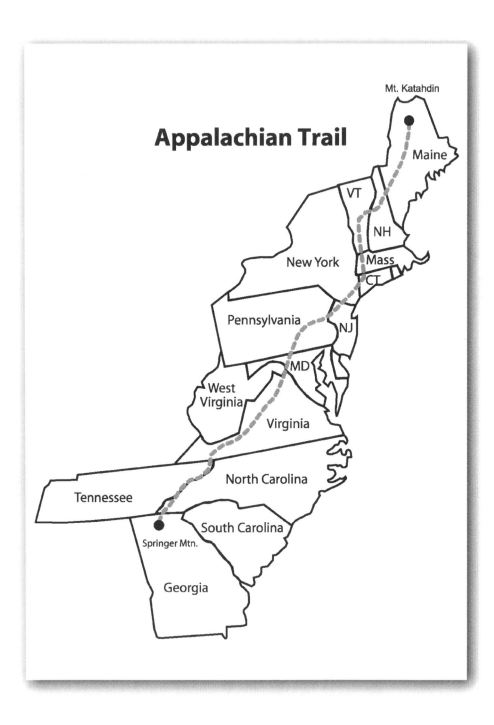

THRU-HIKING

Hiking the entire A.T. within a single year, often times within 5 ½ to 7 months.

    The Appalachian Trail Conservancy web page (www.appalachiantrail.org)

Mike Stephens, "Don's Brother"
Thru-Hiker
March 23, 2013 to September 2, 2013

Introduction

From March 23 until September 2, 2013, I thru-hiked the 2,185.9 mile Appalachian Trail, from Springer Mountain in north Georgia to Baxter Peak atop Mount Katahdin in Maine. Over the 164 day duration of my journey, I only spent 19 nights in the woods. Rather than undertaking a traditional approach to the venture, I chose, instead, to frequent towns often, spending most nights in beds rather than in trail shelters or in a tent. I ate scores of meals at restaurants and often took "town food" back to the trail. Over the course of the five months and eleven days I traveled up the A.T., my system came to be known as the Don's Brother Method, or DBM.

The name for my method relates to my trail name, Don's Brother. The main reason for my hike centered on the illness and death of my younger brother, Don Stephens. Always an exceptionally healthy and athletic man, Don was tragically diagnosed with ALS, or Lou Gehrig's disease, six weeks before his 54th birthday. He died fifteen months later, a little over seven weeks after his 55th birthday. Don was my younger brother by six years.

For as long as I can remember, my brother was always an outdoorsman. He loved to fish and hunt, and from childhood, Don loved the woods. After his diagnosis, I told my brother that I wanted to do something in his honor. A thru-hike of the Appalachian Trail seemed like a good way to memorialize Don and hopefully raise awareness of ALS. Since I would be hiking in Don's memory, I thought an appropriate trail name would be "Don's Brother."

On my journey I wrote about my hike daily and kept an online journal. Many of the entries included references to my brother and an occasional short anecdotal story about his life, especially as it related to the woods. After completing the hike, I edited the journal, added more about Don, and published the work as my first book, *Don's Brother: A Hike of Hope on the Appalachian Trail*. This book deals with Don's story, his faith journey, and how the example of his struggle with ALS inspired a successful thru-hike of the A.T.

In many ways, *The Don's Brother Method* can be viewed as a companion to *Don's Brother*. This method of traversing the Appalachian Trail is not for everyone. If you are one who accepts carrying a heavy pack, and enjoys sleeping in the woods, eating trail food, and rarely showering, this book may not be for you. On the other hand, if you like to hike, but don't care much for camping, it may inspire you to embark on an adventure of your own.

My intention here is not to write a "how to" book, but to give insight on how a "day-hike, thru-hike" can be accomplished. *The Don's Brother Method* is a day-by-day account of how I used my method to get from Georgia to Maine. This second book fills in the logistics of the actual thru-hike and is meant to provide information concerning the practical aspects of attempting a thru-hike. The first book is more memoir; the second book is more instructional.

While my brother was a big outdoorsman, I am not. Don sat and waited for the fish to bite or the deer to amble by. As a competitive marathoner, my time in the woods was spent on the run, with little time devoted to noticing the landscape. Still, nature appealed to me. The outdoors has always been a place I enjoyed being during daylight hours, but I usually wanted to escape inside when nightfall arrived. Embarking on this A.T. adventure, I knew that when I had the opportunity, I would head to town. My only goals were to hike every step north, pass all the white blazes being true to the trail, and not go home until I had finished. How many nights I spent in the woods didn't really matter.

To discover how I accomplished my goals and became a successful thru-hiker of the Appalachian Trail, read on. I'll introduce you not only to the trail, but to many trail towns as well. You'll come to know other hikers I met along the way and some "town folks" that most traditional hikers would never have the privilege of meeting. I'll tell you how I got to and from the trail, where I slept, what I ate, and changes I would make, if I were going to hike the trail again.

I'm not the first to approach the trail in this manner. Therefore, I state again, this is about my hike. There are certainly an abundance of options for traveling up the trail in a similar way. For me, this is how it was done. I hope you enjoy *The Don's Brother Method: How I Thru-Hiked the Appalachian Trail and Rarely Slept in the Woods.*

CHAPTER 1

But I Don't Want to Sleep in the Woods!

*I was a big fan of the "DB method" and if I could of
I would have done my hike that way too.*

JOHN "MISERY" MCCARTHY (BUFFALO, NY)

SITTING AT MY KITCHEN TABLE in late February, 2013, I posed a question for Linda. "Do you really believe I can thru-hike the Appalachian Trail?"

"Of course you can," my wife of thirty-seven years stated encouragingly. Peeking out from behind the morning newspaper, she lovingly continued, "but you can't come home for five months, whether you finish or not."

From the outset I knew that she believed in me. I also felt certain that the "five months" comment was meant to show her support as well as confidence that I could accomplish the task. At least I hoped that's what she meant. For the past ten years she had occasionally heard me talk about a thru-hike. She had watched me read about the trail, saw me researching and ordering gear over the internet, and listened patiently as I outlined my plans. She also knew that it was important for me to fulfill a promise that I had made to my brother Don, before his death the previous August from ALS, or Lou Gehrig's disease.

"I may spend a lot of money," I continued, "because I'm going to find every bed and restaurant remotely close to the trail."

"Do whatever it takes," she replied. "Just have fun."

So there I sat, about one month from beginning an attempt of a thru-hike of the Appalachian Trail, a 2,186 mile "footpath" from Springer Mountain in Northern Georgia to the summit of Mount Katahdin in Maine. As I pondered the enormity of a task that only has about a twenty percent completion rate, I felt a little more confident, knowing that my wife fully approved this endeavor. After all, we were both retired. A check was deposited into my bank account every month. Plus, I had saved over the years. In fact, the more I thought about it, the more I realized that the money I might spend on the trail could quite possibly be less than the money I spent at home. I smiled, remembering that there were places to sleep and eat near the trail that might make the journey more enjoyable. If nothing more, motels and restaurants would certainly make the hike more tolerable.

I hadn't always sought out every eating establishment and hostelry along or in proximity to the A.T. On my first significant section hike in the late spring of 2004, my good hiking buddy, Alton, and I actually tented the first three nights on the trail in Connecticut. Two of those were even at stealth sites. It didn't take me long, however, to tire of those sleeping arrangements. After carrying wet, heavy tents that third day, we were both ready for a bed. In fact, I didn't tent again for the remainder of that ten-night excursion.

What we did do was look for beds. After only three nights in a tent, I spent a night in a private home, one in a shelter, one at a retreat, two in motels, one in a Bed and Breakfast, and the final night on the trail at Bascom Lodge atop Mt. Greylock. I learned early that I could do what I enjoyed, hiking, without doing what I didn't care for so much, sleeping in the woods.

Over the next five years I did tent occasionally. I stayed about an equal number of nights in shelters; however, when the opportunity arose, I sought out a nearby hostel, home, B & B, or motel. A bed or bunk at the end of the day, combined with a hot meal and the option of carrying town food back to the trail for lunch the following day, made the backpacking experience for this hiker much more enjoyable.

Even though I often spent my nights in hostels on or near the trail, or in motels or B & B's in towns near the trail, I always resumed my hike where I had left off the previous day. This was my practice when section-hiking the trail and continued to be the manner in which I travelled on the thru-hike. I may have preferred a bed or bunk over a tent or a shelter, but I was determined to walk past every white blaze in the spring and summer of 2013.

Another thing that I quickly discovered over the years of section-hiking was that my enjoyment of hiking was enhanced by a restful night in town and a restaurant meal. With the need for three to four thousand calories daily, I found it extremely difficult to achieve that rate from trail food. Plus, eating in towns and packing "town food" for the trail allowed me to hike without a stove on the thru-hike. This substantially cut down on the weight of my pack, even when I hiked with it full. I also didn't have to worry about finding fuel or cleaning a cook pot.

So as I prepared for my thru-hike, I was comforted by the thought that there were roads aplenty along many sections of the Appalachian Trail. And somewhere along each of those roads there was an eating establishment and a room with a bed. I would simply have to schedule my hiking day to ensure that I arrived at one of those roads by the end of each day and that I had arranged for a shuttle driver to be there.

Occasionally I hitched to nearby towns; however, I always felt better knowing that a ride waited at the road. On many a less-than-pleasant day on my way to Maine, I more easily dealt with the discomfort with the expectation of a ride, a room, and a meal. Shuttles and motels do cost, so I suppose it would only be appropriate to mention the monetary aspect of a hike like I am proposing.

Comedian Steve Martin included in one of his routines several years ago a line that states, "You can be a millionaire and never pay taxes." He follows that with, "First, get a million dollars." If you plan to try to slackpack most of the Appalachian Trail, first, you need to have a lot of money. "A lot" depends on how many nights are spent in motels rather than hostels and how many meals are consumed in nice restaurants rather than at fast-food establishments. Whether sleeping in a bed or a bunk, and whether eating steak or a burger, you still spend a considerably larger amount of money when following the DBM or Don's Brother's Method, a name that one of my hiking buddies,

Banzai, began calling the plan. You certainly won't need a million dollars; however, you'll most assuredly need a five-figure amount.

My objective here is not to go into exactly how much money I spent on my thru-hike of 2013. Truly, I don't feel that tossing out figures has much relevance since prices change regularly. A motel room that cost me $49 might very well be ten dollars higher the following year. Plus, I stayed in motel rooms by myself exclusively up until I began hiking with Banzai and Pilgrim in Massachusetts. Of course I did share rooms at hostels and in cabins a few times; however, those types of accommodations were less expensive than the typical motel room or B & B. Still, the hiker who shares a room with one or more fellow travelers will obviously spend less.

Those who might consider using the Don's Brother Method should also be strong hikers. In order to end most days at road crossings, distances of oftentimes over 15 miles and sometimes beyond 20, have to be hiked. Having been a competitive marathon runner for over thirty years, I was in good shape when I embarked on my journey. I turned 62 less than two months after leaving Springer. Pretty much all of those who hiked nearby (including the 20 somethings) considered me more than capable of big mileage days, even when carrying a full pack.

Occasionally hostels will be right on or near the trail; however, most are "up the road a ways." The same is true for towns. Sure, you walk right through Hot Springs, NC, Daleville, VA, and Dalton, MA, to name a few, but more often you have to hitchhike or arrange for a shuttle into a town. There are times when several road options are available to access towns. Still, there are going to be many days when a 20 mile hike or longer is needed to reach a desired destination.

For instance, there are only two accessible roads over the 40.1 mile section between VT 9 near Bennington and VT 11/30 leading into Manchester Center. And it's a long shuttle from either. Can it be done? Yes. That's a 20.6 mile hike to USFS Rd. 71 on day one of the stretch, followed by a 19.5 mile hike on day two. Even with a slackpack, these are tough days. Plus, the shuttle from and back to the trail the following day is well over an hour. Again, is it doable? Yes, I did it.

There are also multiple manners in which to handle the food issue. If staying at a motel, I almost always chose one with a complimentary breakfast. There were times that I wanted more, so I often frequented McDonald's or Cracker Barrel if there were one nearby. And I always bought "town food" to take back to the trail for lunch. While traditional A.T. hikers munched a granola bar or partook of peanut butter on a tortilla, I regularly pulled a sub sandwich or a burger out of my pack. In fact, during the course of the 2,185.9 miles I hiked, at various points in the woods, I dined on food from McDonald's, Arby's, Subway, Burger King, Hardee's, Wendy's, DQ, KFC, and on a variety of sandwiches from Delis in proximity to the trail. I even ate McDonald's cheeseburgers that I had packed in while hiking the 100 Mile Wilderness in Maine.

As is quickly becoming obvious, I sought out a bed or bunk in which to sleep, and a restaurant for food, as often as I could find one on my thru-hike of the Appalachian Trail. This method is not for everyone; however, it worked for me.

The adage, "Hike Your Own Hike" is often uttered along the way. I had the utmost respect for those hikers, usually young, who spent most of their nights in the woods and ate mainly "trail food." Most could only afford to do it this way. Still, some, young and old alike, embraced the Don's Brother Method, at least for portions of the trail. Few ostracized those who rarely spent a night on the trail. Again, each person hikes in the manner which best suits him. So here's the way I thru-hiked the Appalachian Trail, along with changes that I would make "if" I were going to hike it again.

CHAPTER 2

Places to Sleep in Georgia

DB's Method got me through four states when I wasn't sure if I could go any further. Sure, I spent more money than I otherwise might have. But, I made it. I completed the trail. I'm not sure if that would have happened had I continued my traditional approach.

Doug "Banzai" Douma (Winston-Salem, NC)

When I, Don's Brother, arrived in Dahlonega, Georgia on March 22, the day before my thru-hike attempt of the Appalachian Trail was to begin, I already had established a general plan for hiking through my home state. Wanting to get off to a traditional start, I figured I would hike the 8.1 miles from Springer Mountain to Hawk Mountain Shelter on my first day and either stay in the shelter or tent.

Arriving at the shelter in the late afternoon, I discovered only one spot was available. With an abundance of what appeared to be good tenting sites, I chose to forego the shelter and spend my first night on the trail in my ten-year-old two-man Eureka Zeus Exo. Even though I had seam-sealed the structure more than once in preparation for my expected five-month adventure, the one-time reliable edifice proved anything but rain-proof.

After finding myself confronted with the task of soaking up standing water inside the tent after an overnight deluge, I quickly determined the once comfortable accommodations were no longer trail-worthy. With a reservation for the second night of the thru-hike at the Hiker Hostel a few miles up Hwy. 60 from Woody Gap, I wondered if the first night in the woods in Georgia could in fact be my last. It wouldn't be, but it could have been.

As I contemplate that wet night on the A.T., I'm reminded I might have arranged for a shuttle from United States Forestry Service (USFS) Roads 42/69 at Hightower Gap, only a half mile farther up the trail from Hawk Mountain. That way I could have easily spent the first two nights in a bunk inside, rather than trying to withstand a downpour in the woods. Hindsight is referenced often on the Appalachian Trail.

On the second day on the A.T. from Hawk Mountain Shelter to Woody Gap, I became aware of my nutritional needs which were not going to be met by consuming trail food exclusively. When I reached the fog-engulfed parking lot at the intersection of GA Hwy. 60 on the afternoon of March 24 I was spent, even though I had only hiked 13.1 miles.

I quickly hitched a ride to the Hiker Hostel, located 6.0 miles east. Staggering inside, I think my first words were, "When is the shuttle into town?"

Since most of the patrons were anticipating beginning their hikes the following day, I was the only one in the capacity-filled lodging who took advantage of a ride into Dahlonega for a meal. Josh, one of the hostel's owners, recognized my depleted state.

"Calorie consumption is maybe the most important thing to consider when trying to thru-hike the A.T.," Josh advised.

A former thru-hiker himself, he offered several nutritional suggestions.

Trying to comprehend, although internally starving, I meekly asked, "How about going through the drive-thru at that Captain D's over there?"

Josh obliged. I ordered the largest dinner on the menu and nibbled on French fries on the drive back to the hostel. Then after devouring the remainder of the four-piece fish meal, my physical and mental states were lifted.

The following morning I was served a full country breakfast at the hostel before shuttling back to the trail at Woody Gap to resume the hike. On a snowy day with patches of ice along the way, I was grateful that I had gotten a good night's sleep in a warm, dry bunk and had eaten two large meals.

Day three on the A.T. took me to the Walasi-Yi at Neels Gap. The hike only covered 10.5 miles; however, due to icy conditions up and over Blood Mountain, I again was grateful for inside sleeping. Apparently others were using the same strategy, at least at this point on the journey, because the hostel bunkhouse, which accommodates 16, was full.

Fortunately there was one spot left in the Blood Mountain cabins, just a short walk up US Hwy. 19 from the outfitter. I was welcomed into the warm, rustic cabin by three young folks who were also in the beginning stages of an attempted thru-hike. When they suggested that I take the loft bed, I humbly accepted the offer, suddenly glad to be in the senior citizen category of this year's thru-hiker class.

Just as I had the night before, I ate heartily, that is if a pizza is considered hearty dining. There was one thing it wasn't, and that was trail food. Unable to consume the entire large pie, I saved a couple of slices for breakfast.

The leftovers, coupled with chocolate milk, donuts, and coffee from the Walasi-Yi, provided me with the necessary energy for the hike to Hogpen Gap, a rather strenuous 6.9 miles, especially considering the lingering icy trail conditions.

Originally I had thought about walking the 21.2 miles from Neels Gap to Unicoi Gap. On a section-hike I had covered the entire distance on the same day in which I had driven four hours from my home to get to the A.T. Since this was only the fourth day of what I hoped would prove a five month journey, I determined that the longer distance with a full pack might not be wise.

The previous evening I had called Doug with Alpine Taxi to arrange for a ride into Helen. Not wanting to risk getting a hitch at GA 348, Hogpen Gap, I decided that this would be my first paid shuttle. On a brutally cold day I quickly knew I had made the right decision. Doug smiled as I feebly attempted to knock some muddy snow from my trail runners before entering his less-than-pristine cab. I smiled too, knowing a warm motel room was in my immediate future.

"Tough hiking today," Doug noted.

"Yeah, really slippery over the ice," I responded.

"I doubt if many will be staying on the trail tonight," Doug continued. "I spent around twelve hours yesterday getting hikers off the mountain and into towns. Been busy all day today too."

With the snow, ice, and sub-freezing temperatures, only a few devout people seemed to be sleeping on the trail. The Best Western in the Bavarian village-themed town of Helen would be where I lay my head for the next two nights. It is one of several reasonably-priced lodgings in the vicinity.

For the first time I employed a strategy which I used often all the way to Maine. I would shuttle into a town a day or two before arriving at the road that the A.T. crossed, leading directly into the trail town. Then the following day, I would shuttle back out to the trail where I had left off and continue the hike north. This also afforded me the opportunity to leave most of my gear in my motel room and slackpack. With only a few articles of clothing, water, and food for the day, I often found myself carrying less than ten pounds.

This method also enabled me to eat a large breakfast to start my day. I began day five by dining in front of a blazing fire in the lobby of the motel. I selected eggs, sausage, bacon, toast, jam, and coffee from the complimentary buffet. Before returning to the trail at Hogpen Gap, I also purchased a sandwich for lunch from the Subway located directly across the highway from the Best Western.

Despite another cold day and a couple of difficult climbs, I hiked enthusiastically, knowing that I would again be sleeping in a comfortable motel room that evening. I also walked with more energy due to the "town food" I was consuming. When I reached Unicoi Gap, I successfully hitched a ride from a tourist back to Helen. For the second consecutive night I treated myself to Wendy's hamburgers, fries, chili, a Dr. Pepper, and a Frosty. I was enjoying my hike without subjecting myself to "trail food" and nighttime frigid conditions within a tent or inside a shelter.

Day six began with a shuttle from Carol, the owner of the Best Western, back to the trail at Unicoi Gap. Even with carrying a full pack, I figured that I could hike all the way to Dicks Creek Gap, US 76, and into Hiawassee. In hindsight this is what I should have done.

Perhaps for a brief moment, I wanted to embrace the elements and be more like the traditional hiker. For whatever reason, I decided to break this section into two days and camp at Addis Gap. After a mere 11.3 miles I strolled down a gravel road to the campsite and pitched my tent next to a few other thru-hikers whom I had met over the past four days. Thus, I spent my second night in the woods of Georgia even though I didn't really have to do so. I could have just as easily walked the additional 5.4 miles to US 76 and arranged a shuttle into Hiawassee.

The following morning, after a restless, cold night on the ground, I quickly hiked those remaining miles to the road. I called ahead to arrange for a ride to the Blueberry Patch from Gary Poteat, a former thru-hiker and the owner of the hostel. Even though there were motels with hiker rates in town, I had looked forward to a night at the Christian-based dwelling.

Later in the afternoon Gary also shuttled other hikers and me into Hiawassee where I dined at an All You Can Eat (AYCE) establishment. Again, I was able to partake of the nutritional foods I needed in order to continue hiking strong. In fact, I enjoyed a late lunch, wrote for about two hours while a pretty waitress regularly re-filled my sweet tea, and then ate again.

The next morning I was treated to an enormous Southern country breakfast of pancakes with fresh blueberry syrup, sausage, potatoes, biscuits, orange juice, and coffee. It boggled my mind that Lennie, Gary's wife, prepared this feast daily, for a donations-only fee. As we bowed our heads as Gary offered up a blessing, I'm sure all were as grateful for their service as I was.

One thing I was becoming aware of as I sought out beds and restaurants, was the number of other thru-hikers who appeared to be doing much the same thing. The Hiker Hostel had been full the night I stayed; no bunks were available at Walasi-Yi; and the Blueberry Patch had also been filled to capacity. I had also noticed a large number of thru-hikers wandering the streets of Helen and a double-figure number devouring the breakfast buffet at the Best Western both mornings I was there. Some were already taking a zero day (no hiking) due to the harsh weather conditions. I don't know how many of the hikers I encountered in Georgia finally made it to Maine; however, I saw only a few after leaving the first of the A.T. states.

As I walked into North Carolina on my eighth day of the hike, I made a mental note of how I had maneuvered my way through Georgia. For the record, I spent two nights in my tent, two in hostels, two in motels, and one in a cabin. I consumed large calorie-filled breakfasts six mornings and restaurant meals four nights. I took "town food" back to the trail for lunch three times. I paid for one ride. On all other occasions I hitched or received complimentary shuttles from and back to the trail.

After only one week on the trail, what would eventually be called the Don's Brother's Method was definitely underway. I was quickly learning that I could indeed thru-hike the Appalachian Trail without having to regularly sleep in the woods.

CHAPTER 3

A Shelter Here; A Hostel There

DB and I spent a particularly miserable day hiking through an ice storm from Burningtown Gap to the Nantahala River. After arriving at the NOC to a hot shower and real food, I began to appreciate the virtue of his method.

Chris "Slim Jim" Spencer (Tampa, FL)

When I headed up the trail from Dicks Creek Gap on a beautiful, sunny Saturday morning, my plan was to stop at Standing Indian Shelter, the second in North Carolina, for the night. Those plans changed, however, after I was informed by a southbound section-hiker that abundant trail magic awaited at Deep Gap, less than a mile prior to the shelter.

Arriving there by late afternoon, and with rain again in the forecast, I reluctantly stopped and set up my tent. It would be the last night that I would utilize the once-reliable, but now leaky, Zeus Exo. Knowing a hotdog supper and an omelet breakfast were going to be provided by a group from Haywood Co., NC, my reluctance to tent slightly dissipated. I figured two complimentary meals would offset the almost certainty of being dripped on in the night.

Using hindsight again, another option would have been to move on to Franklin, NC from Deep Gap at USFS Road 71. This option, however, would have likely required a paid shuttle. The next day I could have been transported back to Deep Gap and walked to Mooney Gap and USFS Rd. 83. From there I would have again gone into Franklin for the night and then back to the trail at Mooney Gap the following morning. This would have left me a little longer hike to Winding Stair Gap, but I would have avoided two nights in the woods.

At the time, I didn't really consider this approach. It would be up the trail near Erwin, TN before I started shuttling into a town two days early, riding back to the same spot where I left the A.T., and continuing the walk north. Nevertheless, if I had started employing the paid shuttles here, I could have stayed four nights at a motel rather than the night in a tent and the next in a shelter.

On Easter morning I again found myself wiping up water from the floor of my tent before stuffing the now much heavier shelter into my pack. I then lined up with a dozen or more thru-hikers to get what was promised to be a 3000 calorie breakfast. At least there was abundant food for anyone capable of consuming that many.

After perusing the menu (yes, there was one), I selected an omelet with ham, cheese and peppers, as well as fresh fruit and a large slice of friendship bread. The "Omelet Angels" even provided a sack lunch. Later in the day I would eat only half of the enormous sandwich, saving the other half and a bag of chips for my evening meal.

By the time I reached the Long Branch Shelter, the first in which I would spend a night, and the last until the Smokies, I was drenched. I didn't really feel that tired or hungry even though I had knocked out 17.1 miles, including the climb over Albert Mountain. Arriving at the shelter to find two spots vacant, I selected the lower level.

While others cooked on camp stoves and dined on various dehydrated dinners, I finished my sandwich and chips, followed by some cookies. Knowing that another motel awaited in Franklin the following day, I didn't even mind my accommodations for the night. In fact, the company was some of the best I would enjoy. The life of a thru-hiker can be good, both on and off the Appalachian Trail.

At daybreak I hastily packed my gear for the short 7.3 mile trek to Winding Stair Gap where I hoped to hitch into Franklin. Folks who assist hikers are often referred to as trail angels. The first of many I would meet along my journey provided the ride to a Microtel. Located just across the street from an outfitter, it seemed the perfect spot. Quickly making note of the restaurants within eyesight, I checked into a room and showered before choosing a Shoney's for lunch. After my meal I walked to a laundromat and then picked up a few items at a nearby drugstore.

The next morning I decided to forgo the rather skimpy breakfast offerings at the Microtel for a large country breakfast at Bojangles'. Then I walked back to the motel to plan my first zero day of the hike. Just as I had encountered in Helen, other thru-hikers lounged on stuffed chairs in the small lobby seating area.

I met Jolly, a hiker originally from England, with whom I would walk over the next few days. He, along with another would-be thru-hiker, Highlighter, asked to share a shuttle back to the trail the following morning. Later in the evening the three of us dined at a steak place adjacent to the motel. Unquestionably, I was eating and sleeping well in Franklin.

While in town I also mailed my tent to a friend back home. Not being very trail-worthy, due to leaks and condensation, the tent no longer met its obligation. At this point in the hike I actually planned to buy a new tent either at the outfitter at the Nantahala Outdoor Center or when I got to Hot Springs. I wanted to first do a little research. Never being what one would consider "very handy," it was important for me to find a tent that I could easily pitch. What one hiker might be able to accomplish within minutes could take me a considerably longer time.

So as I departed Franklin the following morning, I was hiking without a shelter. I wouldn't recommend this part of the method wholeheartedly because one never knows when an emergency may arise. For me, however, the strategy worked in North Carolina and would continue to work for the next 2000 miles.

I headed back up the trail from Winding Stair Gap, tentless, but with an Arby's roast beef sandwich in my pack. Nevertheless, I had a plan. For the past few days I had heard a few others talking about a somewhat-new hostel between Franklin and the Nantahala Outdoor Center. With cold rain in the forecast, I determined that a hostel stay would again be preferable to the woods, so I made a call to the Aquone to secure a bunk.

The Don's Brother Method

While dining on the fast food lunch at Wayah Bald, I shared my itinerary with my newfound hiking buddy, Jolly. He also made a call to get the last spot. When we arrived at Burningtown Gap, Steve, one of the owners of the Aquone, was waiting to drive us to the hostel. Not only would we have comfortable sleeping accommodations, but Maggie, Steve's wife, even offered a full dinner and breakfast at a reasonable price. I again ate and slept well on day twelve of my thru-hike.

Day thirteen took me into the Nantahala Outdoor Center where I shared a bunkhouse with five other thru-hikers. The wooden bunk was not that comfortable; however, I was inside and dry. The NOC offers cabins as well as the bunkhouses. Given the choice again, I definitely would have selected one of the more spacious cabins. I also dined in the evening and the following morning at the River's End restaurant and bought some "town food" for my lunch. All was well as I headed out of the NOC and toward Stecoah Gap.

That night I again found myself in a comfortable bed inside a cabin owned by Phil and Donna, near Robbinsville. Phil also provided the complimentary shuttle from and back to the A.T. Some other thru-hikers, Jolly, and I were also invited into Phil and Donna's home for a modestly priced meal in the evening. I again noted the number of thru-hikers that I was seeing off the trail who, like me, were eating a goodly number of meals at a table and laying their heads on pillows at bedtime. It was beginning to look like I wasn't the only one focused on a hike involving good food, a light pack, and beds.

On day fifteen I let Phil shuttle my gear to the Hike Inn and slackpacked solo from Stecoah Gap to the marina at Fontana Dam. Having pre-arranged for a shuttle to the Hike Inn with its proprietor, Jeff, I walked without worry, knowing that a motel bed was in my future. Not only did I receive the shuttle, but Jeff's wife also drove me, along with three others, into Robbinsville for a meal. I ate at a Mexican place with Piddling Around, a section-hiker from Alabama. I also bought a sandwich, for my first day in the Smokies, before leaving town.

For the next two days I would have no choice but to become the traditional hiker again. Up until this point I had spent consecutive nights on the trail only once. I would repeat back-to-back nights in the woods in the Great

Smoky Mountains National Park where hikers are required to use shelters, if space is available.

When I arrived at Spence Field Shelter on day sixteen I thought about cooking for the first time. It was obvious that my nutritional levels had not been met on this first day in the park. I had not carried a stove the first six days, instead sending it ahead in my first and only re-supply box to the Blueberry Patch. I had carried the unused stove and fuel since then. After a little vacillation, I decided not to break my streak of days on the trail without cooking.

I suffered for the decision on day seventeen, hiking without much energy for much of the afternoon. Still I made it to Double Springs Shelter and a second night in the park. Continuing to exist on foods that required no cooking, I somehow hiked with more enthusiasm the following day to meet friends from home at Newfound Gap.

The Masseys even took me by a Burger King after picking me up before we continued the journey by pickup truck to their condo in Sevierville, Tennessee. I was treated to a steak dinner in the evening, a homemade breakfast the following morning, and even given a sack lunch to take with me back to the A.T.

An additional night awaited in the woods at Tri-Corner Knob Shelter; however, after that I wouldn't spend another night on the trail for over 300 miles. Before saying my goodbyes to the Masseys, I left with them a box of gear that I just wasn't using, including my stove, cook pot, and cup. I was determined to continue for the remainder of the hike stoveless.

At the time I still had plans to purchase another tent or tarp eventually, but I never would. From Newfound Gap at mile 206.8 until I summited Katahdin, 1,979.1 miles up the trail, I hiked without a stove, cooking utensils, and a tent. After all, part of my strategy was a light pack. Mine was getting lighter every day.

After that final night in the Great Smoky Mountains National Park, my hike took me to Davenport Gap where a hostel was situated near the trail. Knowing that I could slackpack with the assistance of one of my former student-athletes, and now friend, Brad Dodson, I easily decided to forgo the hostel for a motel at Lake Junaluska. The accommodations were over thirty miles from the trail, but were near Brad's home in Waynesville, NC. Since Brad had agreed to help me with my plan, I had the opportunity to sleep in a bed for two nights and eat my breakfasts and suppers in restaurants.

On the drive to the motel in Brad's SUV, I again assessed my first twenty days on the A.T. Tonight would make the 6th that I had fallen asleep in a motel. I had stayed in shelters 4 nights, tented 3, and spent 4 nights in hostels, 2 in cabins, and one in a condo. I had received complimentary or free rides or shuttles 16 times, hitched 3, paid for a ride once, and walked from the trail to a bed one time as well.

I was feeling good about my strategy which I had begun referring to as "light pack, big miles, and beds." I had spent thirteen of the first twenty nights inside and had only paid for one ride. I was hiking my own hike and for the most part enjoying it as I headed up an interstate to a bed and a meal just a few miles off the Appalachian Trail.

CHAPTER 4

Over 300 Miles of Beds and Bunks

Throughout my lifetime bucket-list dreaming of thru-hiking the Appalachian Trail, I can honestly admit that my single biggest concern has never involved pain or injury, severe weather, availability of food or drink, crime, crowded shelters, wildlife, or other predictable risks. My inner fear has always stemmed simply from lack of hot water. The Don's Brother Method helps to alleviate that apprehension of too many days without the greatest luxury of all.

LAURA NORRIS (ELIZABETHTON, TN)

WHEN ONE PONDERS THE ENORMITY of the task of thru-hiking the Appalachian Trail, whether at the age of 20 or 60, many questions regarding gear immediately come to mind. To successfully complete a hike of 2,185.9 miles some gear, such as a backpack, is essential. Other items, including a stove, however, are not. On the morning of April 12, my twenty-first day on the A.T., I walked with very little in my pack. I left my sleeping bag, mat, most of my clothes, as well as most of my incidentals in the motel room. With the slackpack, the 21.4 miles breezed by. In fact, I arrived at Lemon Gap, where Brad was to pick me up, over an hour prior to our scheduled pick-up time.

Lemon Gap is where a forest road crosses the A.T., so a hitch from here would be very unlikely. There are some places where a pre-arranged shuttle is absolutely necessary. Hitches, although not always easy, can be managed from many paved road crossings. Forest roads, however, which are usually located in isolated areas, are rarely frequented by vehicles. I never counted on a hitch from a forest road. Still, I arranged to be picked up at a forest road on several occasions.

So after another night in a comfortable room and also after having dined on marginally nutritious, but calorie-filled, town food, I headed back to the trail on day twenty-two with a full pack to walk the 14.4 miles into Hot Springs. My destination was Elmer's Sunnybank Inn, somewhat of a cross between a hostel and a B & B. The 1840 home sits right on the A.T. on Bridge Street.

The day before I had called Elmer to make a reservation. "This is thru-hiker Don's Brother. I'd like a private room, if one is available for tomorrow night."

"Where are you now?" Elmer asked.

"I'm near Max Patch," I stated. "My plan is to end today's hike at Lemon Gap and then hike into Hot Springs tomorrow."

"Call me tomorrow," Elmer stated. "There should be plenty of space."

Early the next morning I again called Elmer, reminding him that I had called the previous day and would like a private room.

"Where are you now?" Elmer wanted to know.

"I'm about two miles north of Lemon Gap," I replied. "I should be in Hot Springs by late afternoon."

"Call when you get closer," Elmer replied. "I think I'll have a room for you."

I was beginning to wonder whether or not a room would be available at the fabled Sunnybank Inn. My backup plan was the only motel in town.

Still I decided to give Elmer one more call. "Elmer, this is Don's Brother again. I'm about two miles south of Hot Springs. Could you reserve a room for me now?" I also mentioned that I would like a private room if one were available.

"I have one room left," Elmer informed me. "I'm putting your name down for it now."

Relieved to know that sleeping accommodations were in my immediate future, I walked with enthusiasm into Hot Springs and up the steps into the

Sunnybank Inn. Elmer greeted me at the door and escorted me to my room, a spacious eclectic abode with two beds. One was strewn with gear from an empty pack that rested on a chair. When I reminded the affable Elmer that I had requested a private room, he smiled and noted, "You're only rooming with one other hiker."

Even though I had to share a room with another thru-hiker, the full-size bed slept comfortably. These accommodations would certainly suffice. The Sunnybank Inn was indeed unique and Elmer was quite hospitable. I was in town and able to partake of a very satisfying meal at the Smoky Mountain Diner, located directly across the street. Sharing the meal and conversation with two young New Englanders, Rocket and Whiskers, made the evening more special.

After a satisfying breakfast served home-style at Elmer's, day twenty-three found me headed out of Hot Springs with another hostel, the Hemlock Hollow Inn off Log Cabin Rd., as my destination. Complete with a short order restaurant, its owners also called the establishment an "outfitter." The meager inventory consisted of a few pieces of gear and a variety of short-term re-supply items. The roomy bunkhouse, complete with a refrigerator and microwave, somewhat made up for the approximate 1.5 mile walk from the A.T.

The accommodations were spacious; however, the clientele on the night I bunked appeared suspect.

"How far are you hiking?" I asked the one of my two bunk mates who in no way resembled a thru-hiker."

"Twenty, maybe thirty miles," the hiker, who had no trail name and refused to identify himself by a given name, replied.

"You mean twenty miles tomorrow?" I inquired.

"No, twenty or thirty miles total," he smilingly replied.

Nameless went on to disclose that he was hiking with a group of four but that he had decided to stay at the Hemlock Hollow Inn for a few days before continuing his hike. I suddenly became very happy that there was one other thru-hiker in the room. Sketchy seems almost an understatement to describe the vagabond with the "Jack Nicholson smile from *The Shining*" countenance.

From sundown until past 10:00 Nameless made multiple trips from the bunkhouse to and from a tenting village that had been erected about twenty yards away. On one return trip, he escorted a lady friend inside. It quickly became obvious what his intentions had been for staying behind when his hiking companions had moved on the previous day.

I wasn't sure if Lady Friend was a hiker or actually resided in one of the tents on a permanent basis. Regardless, the rotund woman with smut marks on her face smiled when I introduced myself. Nameless revealed a pint of bourbon which he shared with the lady. Their giddy laugher failed to awaken the other thru-hiker who had been snoring since sunset.

Lady Friend and Nameless eventually departed one last time to tent city. Before finally succumbing to sleep, I wondered if either would return during the night in a drunken, murderous rage. Neither did. Even though a bit unnerved, I again slept inside in a bunk on night twenty-two. And the sound from a nearby brook even soothed my nerves a bit.

By morning, however, I had determined that what I really needed was a town and a motel. With Erwin still three hiking days in the distance, I made a decision that would prove to be both expensive and providential.

Before leaving Hemlock Hollow I arranged for its owner's son to pick me up that afternoon and shuttle me to Erwin. Failing to do my research, I paid twice the amount that a shuttler from Erwin would have charged. I learned a valuable lesson here. Check more than one service, if more than one is available, before making a shuttle decision.

Still, after an 18.7 mile hike, I finished day twenty-four with a ride into Erwin and took up lodging at the Super 8 motel. I didn't plan it at the time, but I would spend the next six nights in Erwin, yet still hike five of those days. In fact, I stayed so long in Erwin that I made friends with several of the locals, got a massage, and did my laundry twice.

And all this happened while I was covering 105 miles, with a slackpack, and each day returning to that same Super 8 motel room. Plus, every day I carried town food with me for snacks and lunch. The MacDonald's in Erwin earned much of my business over the six days I was there.

Another reason for my trying to avoid sleeping in the woods centered on a serious outbreak of Norovirus. Every year some hikers contract the bug. This year it just seemed to be worse than usual. Two hikers from Germany, who I would hike nearby up until Harpers Ferry, were the first to inform me of the virus.

"Don't sleep in the shelters until past Erwin," Pacemaker warned.

"Many hikers are being forced off the trail they are so sick," Runner-up added.

Later I would discover that the virus seemed to be following hikers up the trail because the sections to avoid shelters seemed to be increasing. First it was up to Erwin, then to Pearisburg, and eventually to Daleville. Since I was still travelling without a tent, towns and rooms seemed to be the only viable option.

Again I'm not recommending this method of thru-hiking for everyone. As I've already stated and will continue to state, it's expensive. Still, for those would-be thru-hikers who prefer hot showers, hot food, and beds to nights in tents or shelters, and for those who have and don't mind spending the money, it's doable.

So after the shuttle into Erwin from Devil Fork Gap I took my second day off. Even though I wasn't hiking, day twenty-five proved to be an eventful one. I met some wonderful folks in Erwin and made shuttle arrangements for the next two days.

My first call on the morning of my off-day was to the legendary Miss Janet. This fine lady ranks among the best of trail angels.

"I need a ride back to the A.T. at Devil Fork Gap tomorrow morning at 7:00, if possible."

"I have other shuttles already scheduled," the kind lady, who has been assisting A.T. hikers for many years, responded. "I can take you at 11:00."

"That's too late. I plan to hike 21.9 miles to Spivey Gap and need an early start."

"That's a two-day hike," Miss Janet advised. "It's going to rain. You shouldn't try that many miles in these conditions. Why not stop for the day at Sam's Gap?"

"I'm a marathon runner and I've already covered a couple of days almost that far."

Laughing, Miss Janet seemed to mumble something about runners.

"I can't take you there at 7:00 anyway, but if you still want to try that stretch in one day, call Tom Bradford."

When I found out that Tom's trail name was "10K," I knew I'd found someone who would understand me. He gladly agreed to provide my shuttle for the following morning.

The next day, day twenty-five, I joined a few other thru-hikers for breakfast. Just like back in Helen, it appeared that many had opted for a night or more at a motel. I shared a table with a hiker whom I had met back in the Smokies, Molar Man, and his wife, Diane. This encounter in the lobby of the Super 8 on the morning of April 17 would prove to be the most significant one of my entire journey. Diane was supporting her husband by meeting him at road crossings with food, and at the end of each day, with a ride to a motel in their Volvo station wagon.

Molar Man had decided to take the stormy day off, which meant that soon we would be at the same place on the trail. I wouldn't have been interested that day; however, when he offered me a shuttle a couple of days later, I had no qualms about accepting his generosity. For today I'd still be walking solo.

Tom promptly arrived at the motel at our pre-determined time. When I asked him how far up the trail he could shuttle me, his reply was one I would hear many times from drivers as I made my way to Maine.

"I'll take you all the way to Katahdin, if you have the money."

So on day twenty-six, I hiked the 21.9 miles (my longest day thus far) from Devil Fork Gap to Spivey Gap. Much of the day's walk was in the rain, yet with a warm room awaiting at the end of the day, not even a couple of falls, nor the lack of any views, detracted from my hiking enjoyment. Back at the Super 8 later that evening, I thought about calling Miss Janet to let her know I had survived the longer day, but I didn't.

The following morning, day twenty-seven, I again used Tom to shuttle me back to Spivey Gap so that I could hike the meager 10.7 miles to the

Nolichucky River. To get from the River (3.8 miles) into Erwin, I used Grim, a shuttle driver employed by Uncle Johnny at his hostel.

When I told the young man that I was trying to stay as few nights as possible in the woods but still thru-hike the trail, he showed little interest in my method. Instead Grim stated that he had thru-hiked a few years earlier and probably only stayed 7 or 8 nights off the trail. For Grim, like many thru-hikers, the trail is where he wanted to be, both day and night.

For me, however, when I wasn't hiking, a town was preferred. Since I had an entire afternoon free, and had by this time decided that this hike was going to be as enjoyable as I could make it, I scheduled myself a massage. Even though I had walked almost 400 miles, the body was feeling good.

On the morning of day twenty-eight I again started my day in the breakfast area of the Super 8. I shared a table with a talkative gentleman about my age who identified himself as 2012 thru-hiker, 5:30. After telling 5:30 that I was trying to stay in rooms as often as possible, he told me that he had used a lot of shuttles on his hike as well. He said I could even slackpack the 100 Mile Wilderness in Maine if I planned meticulously. I would remember 5:30's comments over four months later when I arrived in the last of the 14 states on the Appalachian Trail.

Day twenty-eight proved to also be the first in a while that I didn't have to pay for a shuttle. A local, who had provided a ride from the Food Lion back to my motel on my first night in town, had offered to help me anyway he could while I was in Erwin. Robin, who talked with me about losing his mother to ALS, drove me back to the trail at the Nolichucky River on another overcast morning.

With little on my back, I hiked the 20.6 miles of sloppy terrain in less than nine hours. 10K was already at the road when I concluded today's hike a little after 4:00. Since I had previously planned to accept Molar Man and Diane's offer of a ride the following day, this would be my last shuttle with Tom.

Day twenty-nine, a 14.8 mile hike from Iron Mountain Gap to Carver's Gap, was the first of many days that I would be walking with a hiking companion. Molar Man didn't say much, but from the outset, we seemed to enjoy the company of each other. And I was grateful for the rides. At the end of the day, we rendezvoused with Diane for the drive back to the Super 8, and a final night in Erwin.

The morning of day thirty again found me in the back seat of the Volvo on my way to where we had left the trail the previous day at Carver's Gap. On a very frigid, windy, yet sunny day, Molar Man and I hiked the 18.3 miles over some challenging terrain to Buck Mountain Rd. From there we drove into Elizabethton, Tennessee where we checked into another motel. After a hot shower, I walked to a nearby steakhouse for supper. I was beginning to think that I should add "good food" to the "light pack, big miles, and beds."

Day thirty-one took Molar Man and me from Buck Mountain Rd. to Dennis Cove Rd. Probably at least partially due to a hot, nutritious breakfast, we hiked the 21.1 miles briskly and with few breaks. One thing that I was learning about Molar Man was that he seldom liked to lollygag. For my new hiking buddy, this trek was all business. That suited me just fine, at least for a few days, especially knowing that I had a ride back to the motel in Elizabethton.

That evening as I celebrated one month on my thru-hike I decided, however, that I wanted to get back to hiking solo, at least for a while. With that in mind, I called Warren Doyle at the Appalachian Folk School to reserve a room the following evening. The school is actually Warren's home as well, so the two nights I stayed there I classified as "private home."

Day thirty-two, which took me from Dennis Cove Rd. to Wilbur Dam Rd., would be the last I would hike with the retired dentist from Ohio, at least for a while. After the 13.0 mile day, Molar Man and Diane drove me to Warren's home near Mountain City, Tennessee. Warren only accepts hikers on a "work for stay" basis. Even though I had tried to offer money instead when we spoke the previous evening, the record holder for the most complete hikes of the A.T. flatly informed me that I could work or leave. Spending a few hours moving lumber was the only "hard labor" this almost 62 year-old would engage in for the duration of his hike.

After hiking the 22.6 miles from Wilbur Dam Rd. to Low Gap on day thirty-three, I again had a shower and a room to return to at the Appalachian

Folk School. Warren even suggested that he leave his second car there for me to drive back after I finished the day's hike. We left it at Low Gap earlier in the morning before Warren drove me to Wilbur Dam.

So I added another amenity, at least for the day, to my thru-hike….a car. With my own wheels I was able to drive into Mountain City for a meal. And of course I purchased some fast food from Burger King to take with me on the following day's hike.

The next morning I again awoke in a bed. Since Warren could not return me to the trail where I left off yesterday at Low Gap until around noon, I continued with my "work for stay" duties of moving lumber. Hoisting the two by fours made me long to be back in the woods. I kept thinking, "Walking up mountains is easier than this." I also kept praying that it wouldn't be an injury from manual labor that ended my hike.

Day thirty-four eventually proved to be another landmark one when I reached the Tennessee/Virginia border, marking the entry into my fourth state. Only for a brief moment did I contemplate that it would be over a month before I walked out of it. Even though I hadn't begun today's hike until after noon, I travelled the 15.2 miles into Damascus at a brisk pace, arriving at the Montgomery Homestead Inn several hours before dark.

When I checked into the cozy inn just up the street from the Blue Blaze café, I thought about how fortunate I was to be hiking essentially from room to room. I knew I would eventually return to the woods for a night, but at this point on my journey I just felt glad to be healthy.

In fact, my last night in the woods had been in the Smokies, at Tri-Corner Knob shelter. That was over two weeks ago. Sure, I was spending a lot of money, but I hadn't gotten the Norovirus, I had hiked past every white blaze northbound, and I was meeting some really special people at every stop I made. Life was good on the Appalachian Trail, and in the trail towns as well.

The following day, day thirty-five, presented me with my first negative shuttle experience. From the outset, I was determined to walk every step of my thru-hike northbound, even while using shuttles and slackpacking. When I wanted to use the same room on consecutive nights, like in Erwin, I had arranged for a driver to pick me up at the end of the day's hike, bring me back to town, and then return me back to the trail north of the town the following morning. In Damascus I could find no one willing to do this.

The first shuttle provider I called didn't have any openings. The second said he would take me out to US 58 and let me walk back to Damascus. Many northbound thru-hikers don't mind doing some southbounding during their hikes. I did mind. It was important for me to walk only northward, just because that's how I wanted to do it.

When I departed on March 23 from Springer, there were three promises I made to myself. I would always hike the white blazes unless a detour forced me to adjust my route. I would only hike north and I wouldn't go home until my hike was finished. "Finished" could mean anywhere on the trail for any number of reasons. I hoped "finished" meant at the northern terminus on Katahdin.

If I were to keep these promises, I would have to rely on a hitch back into Damascus at the end of what was to be a 16.7 mile day. The second shuttle driver did say that he would come and pick me up if I could reach him and he wasn't busy. He also added that cell phone service wasn't very good in the area.

For the first time since I had stopped carrying a tent and adopted my bed-to-bed hiking strategy, I was a little worried when I reached US 58 that afternoon. As cars whizzed by at breakneck speeds, it soon became doubtful that I would be able to hitch a ride. So I walked down the highway for over a mile looking for a house where I might use a land line phone to call someone. Two seemingly friendly dogs greeted me by a mailbox.

When I was unable to reach the shuttle service, the residents of the home, Anne and Eddie, seemed to take pity on me. I tried to pay them for the ride they provided back into Damascus, but they refused. They were among the most gracious of the trail angels I would encounter on my walk to Maine. Their generosity helped enable me to enjoy another meal at the Blue Blaze Café as well as an additional night at the Montgomery Homestead Inn. Both provided me with new enthusiasm as I readied myself for day thirty-six.

For a second morning I ate well at Cowboy's, a hiker-friendly establishment along the A.T., before receiving assistance from yet another special person, Journey. The lady from Pennsylvania had rented a car after ending her hike due to injury. Having already completed a thru-hike ten years previously, she was happy to offer this grateful man a complimentary ride back to where the trail crosses US 58.

Before we parted ways, however, Journey urged me to return to the woods, at least occasionally. For a moment I listened, thinking that I might at some time have to forgo the Don's Brother Method eventually. Fortunately, I rarely would.

As I walked up the trail from US 58, I didn't have a clear-cut plan for the night. The only viable outlet was at Massie Gap in the Grayson Highlands. To get to the parking lot at the Gap I would have to traverse a blue-blazed trail for almost a mile at the end of a 14.0 mile A.T. day. This meant, of course, that I would have to begin the next day by walking back up the same blue-blazed trail. To make things more complicated, there wasn't really anywhere to go by road in this remote corner of southwest Virginia, except for a church hostel in Troutdale.

When I finally got cell service I phoned Mary, who along with her pastor husband, Ken, oversees the operation of the hostel. She agreed to meet me at the end of the day's hike. Not knowing any other reliable transportation out of the Grayson Highlands, I was extremely grateful when I located Mary's car.

After arriving back at the church, I repeatedly thanked Mary for her generosity, realizing the distance she had travelled. This would have been a tough hitch since there were few cars in the park on the damp late afternoon.

Even though I was in a bunkhouse with two other thru-hikers, this hostel was several miles from any eating establishment. There were few amenities; however, I was inside. And for the first time since Hemlock Hollow, I was using my sleeping bag and mat on a wooden bunk.

With heavy rain and thunderstorms in the forecast, and not having taken a day off since Erwin, I decided to take a zero and go to church the following day. Not only was this a good decision due to the weather (torrential rain for much of the day), but I was able to participate in a Sunday School lesson and hear an impassioned sermon from Ken on day thirty-seven.

After a second night in my bunk, I arose on day thirty-eight with what I realized would be a difficult task, getting a hitch back to Massie Gap. Knowing that my only hope was to find someone going to work, I arose early, readied my pack, and walked down to the highway, VA 650/16. I was beginning to think that I would never get a ride when a small tan truck stopped.

"Where you headed?" Asked the fortyish man inside who identified himself as Rich.

"I need to get to the log store near the entrance to Grayson Highlands State Park. I'm hoping I can find someone there to drive me into the park and up to Massie Gap."

"Why do you want to get to Massie Gap?"

"I'm thru-hiking the Appalachian Trail."

"The trail is in the other direction," he informed me. "At Dickey Gap."

"That's where I'm hiking to today, to Dickey Gap. I left the trail yesterday at Massie Gap, so that's where I need to continue."

Rich scratched his head and appeared a little puzzled as to why I wouldn't just keep walking from the closest trailhead.

"I need to walk every step of the trail, past every white blaze," I tried to explain. "I'm just hoping that someone at the store will be willing to drive me into the park for $20."

"For $20 I'll drive you," Rich eagerly replied with a smile.

"I'd be most grateful."

When Rich began talking about fishing, I took the opportunity to tell Rich a little about my brother and the reason for my hike.

With genuine compassion in his voice he said, "I've got a mess of fish in a cooler over ice in the back of the truck. Take a couple for tonight. You can cook them over a campfire."

Knowing that I would be back at the bunkhouse, and not particularly wanting to add two frozen trout to my pack weight, I declined. Those fish would have made for some good trail magic.

After Rich dropped me at Massie Gap and reluctantly accepted the $20 I insisted that he take, I again took note of all the fine people I've met whom I would not otherwise have ever crossed paths with, if I were mainly sleeping on the trail. There had already been many and there would be many more in my future.

From Massie Gap I walked back up the blue-blazed trail to the white blazes of the A.T. and headed north. 18.3 miles later I reached Dickey Gap, 2.6 miles from the church hostel in Troutdale. Two other thru-hikers, Not Yet and Sunshine, were trying to hitch when I arrived. After joining them for about fifteen minutes, I decided that they might have better luck as a couple. Wishing them well, I just started walking up the highway.

With every approaching vehicle I paused, stuck out my thumb, and smiled. Unfortunately there were no Riches in small tan trucks on the road this afternoon. After adding the one mile blue-blazed trail back to the A.T. from Massie Gap and the 2.6 miles of road walking back to the hostel, my total mileage for the day was 21.9. Only the 18.3 past white blazes were credited, however.

About five minutes after I reached the hostel, Not Yet and Sunshine arrived. They had finally gotten a hitch. Within minutes we all three landed another ride to the log store and restaurant for a hot meal. The couple who provided that ride even offered to return an hour later for the lift back to the hostel. Once again, there were trail angels in my midst around the small town of Troutdale.

After a final night in a bunk at the Troutdale Baptist Church Hostel, I was transported back to the A.T. at Dickey Gap the following morning by Mary. Not Yet and Sunshine shared the ride. Mary had even prepared small bags with snacks for the three of us. I was undoubtedly blessed on this "town stay" by Mary, Ken, Rich, and all the fine folks of the Troutdale Baptist Church.

From Dickey Gap I hiked a 14.6 mile day to the Mt. Rogers Visitors Center, located off of VA 16. Nearby stands the Partnership Shelter which is popular with hikers because a local pizza place will deliver. In addition to the hot food delivery, the shelter also contains a shower and water spigot. Thru-hikers often spend the night at Partnership, take the shuttle bus service into nearby Marion, VA the following morning, re-supply, and return to the trail to resume their hikes. I had other plans.

Even though I paused for a short break, mainly to admire the shelter's amenities, I decided to hitch a ride into Marion for another motel. The hitch turned out to be one of the worst of the entire hike, but at least I was headed to a room. The driver of the work truck told me he could take me to the edge of town but would have to drop me there since company policy prohibited him from giving rides. What he didn't tell me was that after getting to the "edge" of Marion, I would literally have to walk over two miles to the other side of town to reach the motels.

The heat was overbearing. I was out of water by the time I reached a busy highway and spotted several fast food places. Rather than going immediately to the motel, I stopped at a KFC, lingering over a hot meal in the air-conditioned restaurant. Then it was on to the Econo Lodge where I booked a room for two nights. Noticing Molar Man and Diane's white Volvo in the parking lot, I stopped by their room to say hello. Later in the evening I did laundry, had another hot meal, and even bought some fast food for tomorrow's lunch on the trail. Then contentedly, I ended day thirty-nine back in a bed.

After a complimentary breakfast at the Econo Lodge, I joined Not Yet and Sunshine for the shuttle bus ride back "up the mountain" to VA 16. Day forty took me to US 11/VA 653 near I-81. Good fortune awaited at the end of this day when Molar Man and Diane stopped at the intersection to give me a ride back into Marion. They even offered me a ride back to the trail the following morning.

Day forty-one would be a special one for many reasons. The most noteworthy was that I would be sleeping on the trail for the first time since the Smokies. Due to several factors, I had hiked over 350 miles without spending a night in the woods. Without a doubt, my "light pack, big miles, and beds" method was working. I was hiking strong, eating and sleeping well, and pretty confident that I could make it to Maine.

CHAPTER 5

Avoiding the Virginia Blues

A long distance hike is your personal journey. I am personally in favor of sleeping on the trail, whether it be in a shelter or tent because it helps me embrace the whole wilderness experience. I stayed at both hostels and hotels along the AT and would prefer hostels for the social aspect more than for budget. I love meeting people and hearing their worldly stories.

MIKE "ROCK STEADY" JURASIUS (SAN LUIS OBISPO, CA)

MANY WHO ATTEMPT A THRU-HIKE of the Appalachian Trail end their journey somewhere in Virginia. This state with the largest number of miles, over 550, can pose more psychological problems than physical ones, with even experienced hikers succumbing to the mind games encountered in the Old Dominion state.

There are physically demanding sections of Virginia. There are also less challenging sections. These easier (although "easy" isn't a word that really ever applies to the A.T.) sections of trail can provide opportunities for hiking faster and farther. By this stage of the trek, most thru-hikers are well-conditioned. I often found myself doing 20 or more miles a day, even with a full pack in Virginia. Thankfully, my ability to find beds kept me mentally in the game as well.

However, after four to six weeks of doing the same thing every day, many hikers grow weary of the monotony. They miss loved ones. They realize that they still have three to four months before they will reach Katahdin. They begin to think about what they could be doing elsewhere. Their bodies are tired, battered and bruised, and they just may want to return to some normalcy in life. Fortunately for me, at this point in my thru-hike I was still doing pretty well, both physically and psychologically.

On day forty-one I departed Marion, once again with a full pack, including Arby's roast beef sandwiches for my evening meal. I also began the day with the ambitious goal of hiking 23 miles to the Chestnut Knob shelter. I reached my destination just before sundown; however, this had been one of my most challenging days, mainly due to the pack weight and high mileage. Still, I actually felt happy knowing that I wouldn't be paying for a place to sleep.

Later in the week, Paisley, a young lady thru-hiker I had first met in Tennessee, would tell me I couldn't count Chestnut Knob as a shelter since it had four walls and a door. When arriving I just felt relief that there was space available so late in the day. Among the eight in the shelter, All the Way, a 66 year-old ex-military man, and young Shrek were the only thru-hikers. I would hike some with both the next day and later hike with and around All the Way in sections of New Hampshire and Maine.

After a fairly good night's sleep at Chestnut Knob, the hike into Bland on day forty-two almost proved disastrous. To begin with, my breakfast of a couple of snack cakes was ill-advised. With very little in the way of nutrients in my body, I was struggling mightily by early afternoon. At one point, I even thought about laying out my mat and sleeping bag on a picnic table and spending the night under the stars.

Not only was I suffering physically, but my emotional state was in somewhat of a shambles as well. Even my first bear sighting didn't alleviate the doldrums. The final 6 miles of the 21.7 mile hike into Bland could easily be considered in the top 5% of difficulty of my entire thru-hike, largely due to my depleted state.

In hindsight, splitting this 44.7 mile section into three days would have helped conserve my dwindling energy. There are two roads (VA 742 and VA 42) where I could have cut the first 23.0 mile day short and shuttled back to Marion for a third night. If I had stopped at VA 42 and shuttled back to Marion, the following day I could have stopped at VA 623 and then shuttled ahead to Bland. This would have allowed me to slackpack two of the three days and again eliminate the night on the trail. The itinerary would have given me days of 11.8, 17.2, and 15.7. Only day two of the three would have necessitated a full pack.

Hindsight aside, when I did finally reach US 52, 2.5 miles east of Bland, VA, I was beyond exhausted. Fortunately, I was able to reach Bubba, a local shuttle provider, by cell phone. When he pulled up in his somewhat dilapidated truck, darkness approached. Before dropping me off at the motel, Bubba and I also arranged a time for a shuttle back to the trail the following day. He would also provide a shuttle at the end of the next day's hike. This enabled me to slackpack and spend an additional night in Bland.

After checking in at the Big Walker Motel, a comfortable "mom and pop" business, I ventured across the road to the closest fast food restaurant, a DQ. Two chili dogs, a large burger, fries, a coke, and a chocolate shake helped to replenish most of my drained calories. It wasn't the healthiest of meals, but it served its purpose.

Just after sunrise, I made another appearance at DQ for breakfast. Bacon, pancakes, and coffee replaced the snack cakes I had dined on yesterday. With a full belly and a slackpack, I headed back up the trail at US 52 after being dropped off by Bubba. Knowing that I had a room to return to at the end of the day, and carrying a foot long DQ hotdog for lunch, I smiled throughout most of the day.

When I reached VA 606 I walked the half-mile up the road to Trent's Grocery, Bubba's designated pick-up spot. Shrek, the young lad from Washington State, had walked to the grocery as well. Before heading back to Bland, Bubba provided Shrek with a ride back to the trail crossing. Day forty-three ended with another night at the motel in Bland and another DQ supper.

I began day forty-four with breakfast at Subway, a short walk up the highway from my motel. From there I again shuttled back to the trail in Bubba's truck. With replenished strength and renewed enthusiasm after two nights in a motel, I hiked 13.9 strong miles. Today's trail took me from VA 606 to Sugar Run Rd. and Woods Hole Hostel.

Earlier in the day I had called the hostel and spoken to Neville about bunk space. She told me that the bunks were on a first come, first served basis, but that I could reserve a bed in a shared room in the main house. When I arrived, however, I chose the one available private room. Since I really didn't have budget concerns, I made my decision on the side of comfort. And it proved to be a good one. The bed at Woods Hole was the most comfortable I had slept in the entire hike. No other bed would rival it all the way to Millinocket.

After eight hours of uninterrupted sleep, I awoke to the pattering of raindrops on the tin roof. I was not deterred by the rain, wanting to make it to Pearisburg by early afternoon. So after a plentiful breakfast served family style in the company of several other thru-hikers, I walked a wet 10.4 miles on day forty-five to the outskirts of Pearisburg. From the trail I scored a ride into town from Snail Mail, a section-hiker that I had met earlier in the day. He had left his truck in a grassy field near the trail.

I thanked my new friend and wished him well before walking into the closet-like office of the Plaza motel.

"I'm Mike, Don's Brother. I called about a reservation earlier today. I need a room for two nights." I again had planned to walk north a day, and shuttle back to Pearisburg for a second night in a bed.

"We have a three night hiker special," she offered. "It's only a few dollars more than two nights."

This was too hard to resist. I knew that there was a reliable shuttle provider in Pearisburg. I also knew that there were roads where I could be driven back to town for that additional night. In fact, with a couple of fairly long shuttles, I realized that I could cover the section between Pearisburg and Daleville without a single night in the woods.

"I'll take the three nights," I stated after thinking about my decision for about five seconds.

I walked to my room, showered, and then proceeded to a Mexican restaurant across the road from the motel. After two chicken quesadillas and rice, I ventured over to a Dairy Queen on the opposite side of the highway for ice cream. Then it was back to my room. Although in no way resembling the hotel at the corner of 5th Avenue and East 59th Street in Manhattan, this Plaza provided an adequate base.

The following morning I walked to Hardee's for breakfast. Good fortune again surfaced when an older gentleman engaged me in conversation about my hike. Fred Austin, a retired Methodist minister and superintendent, offered the one-mile ride back to the A.T. I would see the kind-hearted Christian the next two mornings when dining at Hardee's as well.

Knowing that I would again be sleeping in a bed for three nights in Pearisburg, and quite possibly for at least the next week, the steady, cold rain that I faced on the morning of day forty-six couldn't damper my spirits. Not only did I cover the 21.7 miles from Pearisburg to VA 635 in less than nine hours, but I also met a section-hiker on the trail, with whom I arranged to share a ride over the next two days.

On day forty-seven, Speck, the section-hiker I had met the previous day, and I shuttled back to the trailhead at VA 635 with a Pearisburg resident named Don. Don also arranged to pick us up in the afternoon and shuttle us back to the trail the following morning. Speck and I hiked together all day, covering the 13.1 miles from VA 635 to a graveled VA 601 at Rocky Gap by early afternoon.

Before dropping me back at the Plaza, Don detoured by Wendy's so that Speck and I could catch a late lunch. My large chili and burger were much appreciated after again hiking in a steady rain for most of the day. I don't know which felt better, the hot fast food, or the hot shower that I enjoyed a little later.

For a second consecutive evening I dined from a Mexican menu and followed my meal with a DQ dessert. Several other thru-hikers mingled in the dairy bar on the cold, wet evening. Several were amazed that I had only spent one night in a shelter since the Smokies.

After three consecutive days of steady rainfall, blue skies and bright sunshine greeted Speck and me as we returned to the trail at VA 601 on day forty-eight. We said goodbye to Don for the final time before embarking on a 16.8 mile day which would take us to Craig Creek Rd., VA 621. It was here that Speck had arranged for a shuttle into Daleville from her son's fiancé, Jodi, who was kind enough to provide me with a ride as well.

I checked into the Howard Johnson motel where many other thru-hikers were taking a respite from the trail. At the time I didn't know; however, over the next ten days the Daleville/Troutville area would be my base. Six of the nights I had planned. The other four were due to the only significant injury I would sustain over the entire 2,185.9 miles from Springer to Katahdin. In fact, before I departed from this area, I would sleep in three different motels, shop at Kroger four times, and have meals at over a half-dozen restaurants. I would also meet close to one-hundred other hikers who were also enjoying the luxuries of a town for a day or two.

On day forty-nine I joined Speck and Jodi for a ride back to the trail at VA 621 with Homer, a local shuttler who had thru-hiked the trail with his wife and two young children in 2003. Speck and Jodi planned a three day hike with two nights in the woods from VA 621 to Daleville. My plan was to hike the 15.4 miles to Newport Rd., VA 624, and get a shuttle from Homer back to Daleville. I made it to the road that evening just as the rain began around dusk. Happily for me, Homer was already at the trailhead.

With 696.8 miles of the A.T. complete, I scheduled my fourth day off in Daleville. Had I known at the time that three days later I would be taking four consecutive days off, I would have forgone this one. Nevertheless, day fifty allowed me to do laundry, have a bent trekking pole replaced at a local outfitters, and visit with other thru-hikers who were lodging in town.

After my day off, Homer again shuttled me back to the A.T. at Newport Rd. My ambitious day proved to result in a minor setback for a couple of reasons. On a section-hike of this portion of trail back in 2009, I had taken three days to cover the 25.6 miles from Newport Rd. to Daleville. On day fifty-one of my thru-hike I planned to slackpack this section in one day. Even though there were some minor challenges around McAfee Knob and Tinker Cliffs, my downfall came from my shoes.

Since day one of my hike I had been wearing size 10.5 Brooks Cascadia trail runners. I began hiking today in my second pair after putting almost 700 miles on the first. What I didn't realize was that my feet had flattened somewhat. Foolishly, I hiked the long day in very tight shoes which eventually led to an Achilles issue. Three days later I would be sidelined in a motel room icing the injury and taking a high-powered anti-inflammatory.

Before the total breakdown occurred, I was able to enjoy sharing day fifty-two with Speck and Jodi. The A.T. often crosses the Blue Ridge Parkway throughout much of Virginia. Today we covered the section from Daleville to Harvey's Knob Overlook at the Parkway's 95.3 mile marker. At the end of the 16.1 mile day, Homer again provided the shuttle back to Daleville. By now I had moved from the Howard Johnson across the road to the Super 8, a much nicer motel at the same price.

From the outset on the following morning, I knew things weren't going to go as planned. With a full pack in tow, my original destination was the Bryant Ridge shelter. After eleven consecutive nights in a bed, I had decided to save a few dollars and return to the woods for a couple of nights. I would enjoy the spacious Bryant Ridge shelter eventually; it just wouldn't be on the evening of day fifty-three.

Less than three miles into what had been scheduled as a 15.9 mile day, the soreness in the Achilles returned. What started as a mild ache quickly developed into a sharp, burning pain. As my hiking partners slowly disappeared in the distance I found myself moving with a distinct limp. Somehow I managed to get to the Cove Mountain shelter where Speck, Jodi, and some section-hikers had stopped for lunch.

It was here that I was forced to change my plan. Realizing that the injury needed treatment, I used my cell phone to call Homer. He said he could pick me up at Jennings Creek for a ride back to Daleville. Those last 3.2 miles from Cove Mountain to VA 614/Jennings Creek were excruciating. My Achilles throbbed with every step. I paused often to take the pressure off the ankle before limping on toward the road.

Homer showed genuine concern as I gingerly stepped into his car. He even offered to loan me a vehicle for the days I would be resting. I graciously declined, knowing that I would be spending most of the next few days indoors.

Days fifty-four through fifty-seven found me back in Daleville. I returned to the Super 8, and even secured the same room for the first two nights.

When the clerk told me the room rate was going to double over the weekend, due to a college graduation, I moved to the neighboring town of Troutville. Even though this location is slightly farther away from the trail, my restaurant choices actually increased with a Shoney's and McDonald's only a few yards away.

After four days of rest, enough ice to fill a bathtub, more than a healthy dose of Celebrex, and a greatly diminished bank account, I was again ready to hike. I decided to wait, however, until after lunch to resume the hike on day fifty-eight. This time it was Homer's son, Bennett, who shuttled me back to the A.T. at Jennings Creek.

Since I wanted to make sure the Achilles was well enough to hike, I only planned a 3.8 mile day with the Bryant Ridge Shelter as my destination. I was also wearing a different pair of new shoes. They were still the Brooks Cascadia. Upon resuming my trek, however, I switched to a size 11.0. It proved to be a wise decision.

Even though I chose a night on the trail, I could have easily arranged a shuttle from BRP mile 76.3, 13.7 miles north of Jennings Creek. Since I had just spent the previous sixteen nights in beds, and since I didn't want to hike that far on my first day back, the shelter was a better choice. I hadn't really altered my philosophy of "light pack, big miles, and beds." A change just seemed to be more sensible on this evening.

When I awoke in the shelter on day fifty-nine, the Achilles felt fine. Still not wanting to go too far, I ended the hike after only 10.2 miles at the Thunder Hill Shelter. The company was good on a rather warm, sticky night; however, the accommodations left much to be desired. A few hundred mosquitoes made matters worse. This would be the last time that I would spend two consecutive nights in the woods for the duration of my hike, including the 100 Mile Wilderness in Maine.

The following morning the Achilles continued to feel fine. I covered the 14.6 miles from Thunder Hill to US 501, VA 130 in less than seven hours. In fact, because I arrived much earlier than I had expected, Ken, the shuttle driver I had contacted, had not arrived. When I was offered a ride to Buena Vista by a tourist, I called and cancelled the shuttle. Day sixty ended in another town, Buena Vista. The Budget Inn on US 60 would provide the bed for the next three nights.

Before arriving in Buena Vista I had gotten in touch with another former student-athlete whom I had coached. Deidra Dryden not only provided three shuttles while I was in town, but also invited me to join her family for home cooked meals on two of the evenings. Once again, I was treated to a special and memorable town experience.

On day sixty-one I continued to "nurse" the Achilles, only hiking 10.8 miles to where the trail crosses the Blue Ridge Parkway at mile marker 51.7. This time I did contact Ken for the ride back into town.

Then on day sixty-two I continued from the BRP marker to US 60 which leads into Buena Vista. Those 11.0 miles were among the least difficult in Virginia. Had I not still been a little concerned about the Achilles, I could have easily hiked the entire 21.8 miles from US 501 to US 60 in one day and saved a night's lodging.

After a third breakfast at the Burger King across the street from the motel in Buena Vista, my final shuttle back to the trail with Deidra began day sixty-three. On an unseasonably cold day, I hiked 16.3 miles from the trailhead at US 60 to Spy Rock Rd.

When I called innkeeper Earl the night before to make a reservation at the Dutch Haus B & B, he warned me about the extremely rocky mile-long road leading to a gravel road where he could pick me up. As I attempted to avoid stepping on sharp, pointy rocks, I simply reconciled that this was similar terrain to what I would encounter in Pennsylvania. Feeling uneasy being on an unmarked side trail, I breathed a sigh of relief when I spotted his vehicle.

The short drive in the heated car gave my fingers a chance to thaw. Several other hikers lounged in the inn that Earl operates with his wife, Lois, near the town of Montebello. Once again, it appeared that I wasn't the only one looking for a night away from the woods.

The meals I received at the Dutch Haus were outstanding. Even though I had to begin day sixty-four with a difficult walk back up Spy Rock Rd. to reach the A.T., the breakfast more than made up for having to face this obstacle.

With the nutritious meal under my belt, I hiked strong all day, including the climb up the Priest, the tallest mountain on the A.T. in Virginia.

Along the way today I met Banzai for the first time. When I told the 30 year-old engineer from Michigan that I was getting a shuttle back to the Dutch Haus, he immediately asked to join me. After suffering bitter cold in his tent the previous night, Banzai was in definite need of some warm accommodations. Our paths would cross again in New York and Connecticut. My new friend would eventually adopt my method and become a hiking partner from Great Barrington, Massachusetts to Mount Washington, NH.

When Banzai and I reached the Three Ridges Overlook, mile marker 13.1 on the Blue Ridge Parkway, Earl waited for the ride back to the Dutch Haus. With another slackpack and good company, I was only pleasantly tired after the challenging 20.3 mile day. The hearty meal and fellowship back at the B & B once again reinforced my strategy of "light pack, big miles, and beds."

CHAPTER 6

Shenandoah Snoozing

As long as you're respectful of the trail and other hikers, I don't think there is a wrong way to hike the A.T. If I had had the money, I would have been doing the same thing DB was.

VANESSA "FINDER" RICHARDS (SEATTLE, WASHINGTON)

ON THE MORNING OF DAY sixty-five, Earl drove Banzai and me back to the trail at the Three Ridges Overlook. Within a short time Banzai hiked ahead. It would be one month later in New York before I would see Banzai again. Anxious to get to Rockfish Gap, the southern terminus of the Shenandoah National Park, I walked 18.8 miles on a rather warm day, arriving at the Gap by mid-afternoon. A section-hiker I met and hiked with throughout the day, Brass Rat, offered to share his shuttle. Since I again wanted a comfortable room for the night, I decided to accept his offer for a ride a couple of exits up I-64.

Several eating establishments, including a Cracker Barrel and Applebee's, were located a stone's throw away from the Super 8 where I had decided to lay my head for the next two nights. Before leaving the trailhead near Rockfish Gap, I had secured a list of shuttle drivers in the area. Waynesboro is known as one of the trail-friendliest towns on the A.T. Jim and Cindy verified that label when they arrived at my motel the following morning. Without accepting any money, they shuttled me back to the trail.

The Don's Brother Method

When I explained my method of hiking to Jim, he reserved judgment, agreeing to pick me up later that afternoon along Skyline Drive so that I could spend another night at the Super 8. The Blue Ridge Parkway, which parallels the Appalachian Trail from north of Daleville, becomes Skyline Drive when the A.T. enters Shenandoah National Park. Similar to the BRP, the trail crosses the Drive numerous times as it winds through the park.

My plan for day sixty-six was to have Jim meet me at the Riprap parking area at Skyline mile marker 90.0. Realizing that I would arrive there well ahead of the pre-arranged time, I phoned Jim to change the pick-up point to Black Rock Gap. My first day in the park, a 19.1 mile slackpack, ended with a ride back to a comfortable motel room, where I enjoyed a hot shower followed by a steak dinner later that evening at a Logan's Roadhouse.

After a restful night's sleep at the Super 8, I ventured over to Cracker Barrel for breakfast before Jim arrived at the motel to drive me back up to Black Rock Gap. Before saying goodbye to my Waynesboro friend, I insisted that he take a little shuttle money, at least to cover the price of gas. I doubt that many thru-hikers shuttle back to the Waynesboro area after one night in Shenandoah National Park. For me, however, the strategy worked well. Preparing to spend my first night in the woods after a week of beds, I felt grateful to be healthy and hiking strong.

I was also looking forward to taking advantage of the waysides within the park. Throughout the Shenandoahs, a series of waysides, or restaurants, are located just off the trail. Already having section-hiked this portion of the A.T. in 2006, I knew that I could purchase my lunch on the trail for the next few days. My first dining experience occurred at the Loft Mountain Wayside around noon on day sixty-seven. A small group of thru-hikers congregated outside, and more were already inside enjoying the air-conditioned facility. I ordered a rather expensive burger, fries, and a soft drink.

With a full stomach and hiking somewhat sluggishly, I altered my scheduled plan. Instead of completing what would have been an ambitious 25.5 mile day with a full pack, I decided once again to utilize one of the A.T. shelters for the night. Actually in Shenandoah National Park the structures are referred to as huts. Regardless of the name, my night was spent in the company of two section-hikers from France at the Pinefield Hut after a 13.9 mile day. I wasn't in a bed, but I actually slept quite comfortably.

Again I had no desire to stay in the woods on back-to-back nights. On the morning of day sixty-eight I packed quickly, vacating the hut before 6:30. Most days I had a definite plan prior to beginning my hike. Today I modified the plan. After 11.6 miles I arrived at Swift Run Gap at US 33 just after 12:00. Unable to hitch a ride into Elkton for lunch, I phoned a local motel to check on a shuttle. A few minutes later, Bob arrived at the intersection on Skyline Drive with his dog, Shadow.

Bob was so hospitable that a new plan occurred to me. "If I spend a night at your motel, could you take me back to the trail today and let me slackpack to the Lewis Mountain Campground?" I asked Bob as we drove into Elkton.

Bob was happy to oblige after he first stopped by a DQ for me to pick up some burgers. Then after I checked in at the Country View Motel, Bob returned me to the trail so that I could hike an additional 8.3 miles to give me a 19.9 mile day. Shortly after completing the hike near the campground, Bob and Shadow appeared for the return shuttle to the motel.

The Country View consists of a series of free-standing rooms. The one I occupied was clean and comfortable. If I had been able to arrange a ride back from farther up the trail, I would have spent a second night. Unfortunately, I couldn't locate another shuttle provider in the area. When Bob said he really didn't want to drive that far, I opted to hike on to Skyland on day sixty-nine.

Like the previous two days, I was able to have a hot lunch near the trail. Today's dining establishment was Big Meadows, a combination lodge, campground, and wayside. After a lengthy break and a substantial lunch, I completed the 16.6 miles to Skyland by mid-afternoon. Alton and I had stayed a night at the resort back in 2006, so I expected the room to be expensive. I also planned to do a little begging to get the price down.

Even though I had only slept on the trail once in the past nine days, I imagine I still appeared rather haggard as I entered the office of Skyland.

"What's your rate for a thru-hiker?"

Looking at me as if she didn't know the term, the trying-to-sound-cheerful clerk replied, "Our rate for a room is $$$$ a night."

"Whoa, $$$$ a night," I mumbled under my breath. As I went into my negotiation posture, a couple, with a pre-adolescent child, peered perplexedly in my direction. I smiled at the child when she asked her parents if I were homeless.

Looking back at the clerk, I continued, "I'm a thru-hiker. Many places on the trail offer special rates. I've walked all the way from Georgia."

Realizing that I wasn't going to just go away, the young lady said that she would check with her manager. While she was away I removed my pack and stretched a bit. After a few minutes an older woman with pleasant countenance appeared. The other couple and their daughter leafed through some vacation brochures as I negotiated. They appeared to have lost interest in the homeless hiker.

"The best rate I can offer you is $$$ for a motel room for the night. All of our cabins are full."

By now the younger pair had regained interest. An elderly couple (meaning probably over 80) had also entered the office and overheard my plea.

"Could you please check with someone else to see if there's any way you could offer a lower rate to a thru-hiker?"

I'm not sure if the lady really called anyone; however, she appeared to be in a conversation. After about two minutes she put down the phone, smiled, and said, "My very best and last offer is $$."

I briefly thought about continuing to barter. But then I realized that the lady had reduced the room rate substantially. That was awfully generous of her, and I appreciated that she genuinely seemed to want to help me.

"This is the most expensive room I've stayed in on the entire hike, but I'll take it," I stated, even trying to appear grateful. Actually I was. A leaflet I had picked up back at Lewis Mountain Campground had indicated that the lowest priced room this time of year was over $$$$. Still, when I reviewed my expenses after completing my hike, this was by far my most expensive night "on" the Appalachian Trail. If I had planned better, perhaps I could have found other hikers who may have wanted to share a cabin with me. Of course this would have meant calling ahead for a reservation.

Another option which I didn't attempt here would have been to hitch a ride on Skyline Drive to Luray, VA. I then could have slackpacked from

Skyland the following day to US 211, which is nine miles east of Luray. This plan would have afforded me the opportunity to stay two nights in the same room at about the same rate as one night at Skyland.

Despite the rather exorbitant rate (at least by thru-hiker standards) the sunset that evening rivalled any I have ever experienced. Another good thing about Skyland was the restaurant. After a hot shower I proceeded to the tap-room for some more "town food." Three section-hikers, whom I had met earlier in the afternoon, occupied a table across the room, but there were no thru-hikers dining at Skyland on this night.

As day seventy began my pre-determined destination was Elkwallow Gap, a starting and finishing point when I had section-hiked the Shenandoahs in 2006. I called Mike, the owner of the Terrapin Station Front Royal Hostel, concerning a shuttle from the gap so that I could stay two nights at his establishment and slackpack the following day. On an extremely hot and humid day, I carried a full pack 18.3 miles.

Arriving with Mike at the hostel, I found only one other guest. I had read some of Pilgrim's online journal entries; however, this would be my first encounter with the 66 year-old hiker from southern California. Pilgrim had started over two weeks before me, but I knew that we had been near each other for some time, based on shelter log entries. What I didn't know, as we dined at a Mexican restaurant later that evening in Front Royal, was that Pilgrim would eventually become an integral part of the Don's Brother's Method of hiking the Appalachian Trail. Even though Pilgrim was a day farther up the trail from me, I would see him again two nights later at the Bears Den Hostel.

Before Bears Den, however, there was day seventy-one and a 19.1 mile slackpack from Elkwallow Gap to US 522, four miles east of Front Royal. Mike drove me back to yesterday's ending location just after dawn. With some of the flattest terrain over the past week, the miles passed quickly. The town food I had packed in for the day kept my energy levels high, even though my enthusiasm for hiking was diminishing. Despite the town food and beds, the hike had becoming drudgery. I was beginning to understand why would-be thru-hikers often dropped out in the seemingly endless state of Virginia.

For me this day concluded with another night at Terrapin Station. In hindsight I might have chosen otherwise. In fact, for the thru-hiker looking for a bed near US 522, there are numerous options. Only a stone's throw from the intersection of the trail and road, Mountain Home Bed and Breakfast sits just off the road. I would highly recommend this facility which is owned and run by Possible, a former thru-hiker who is renovating the old homestead on the same acreage. There are also a few modestly priced motels in Front Royal. Hitching seems pretty easy along this route as well.

The following morning, day seventy-two, I was able to slackpack for another day, thanks to Mike. He agreed to meet me at Ashby Gap at the end of the day with my gear and then drive me to Bears Den Hostel where I planned to set up a base for the next two days. So after a fairly comfortable 20.0 mile day, I arrived at the gap just as a light rain began to fall. Thankfully, Mike was waiting. Otherwise, I would have gotten soaked since within a couple of minutes the sprinkle turned into a flash flood.

I had stayed two nights at Bears Den on my section-hike of the area; therefore, I knew about the hiker special. For $30 folks receive a bunk, a shower, laundry, a pizza (which you bake yourself), a soft drink and a pint of ice cream. It's one of the best bargains on the entire Appalachian Trail.

Although still a trail day ahead of me, Pilgrim was also enjoying the amenities of Bears Den. We shared our itineraries in the common area before turning in for the evening. Pilgrim appeared somewhat puzzled when I told him how I had arrived at the hostel today. My extensive use of shuttles seemed a little foreign to him. As he listened to my plans for the next few days, a wry smile appeared in the corner of his white-bearded mouth.

"So while I've been looking for campsites and shelters, you're focusing on roads?" Pilgrim questioned with a hint of incredulity.

"That's right. I'm trying to hike from road to road as often as I'm able. I got off the trail at Ashby Gap today. Tomorrow I'll shuttle back there and hike here. Since I'll already have a bunk, I can leave most of my gear here and slackpack."

Pilgrim smiled again, shaking his head. At the present time, I wasn't sure how he really felt about my hiking strategies. I didn't know if he admired my ingenuity or was cursing me from within because I was avoiding nights in the woods whenever possible. However he felt on the evening of June 2, a little over a month later he would be embracing my method and become a hiking partner all the way to Maine. Obviously, neither of us knew this at the moment.

Before turning in for the night I made arrangements with one of the hostel's caretakers for a shuttle back to the trail. John indicated that he could drive me at 7:00 the following morning. What he didn't tell me, however, was that he wouldn't be able to return me to exactly where I had ended the previous day's hike.

"This isn't the right place," I informed the teenager, who obviously knew the area, as he pulled his car into a dirt parking lot. "It's back on the road," I continued.

"I can't pull off there," John stated. "It's too busy and dangerous. It's only a short piece that you're missing. Just start from here."

"No, I can't do that," I said with a smile, as I began walking in the opposite direction.

So since my drop-off was actually a quarter mile north of Ashby Gap, I had to hike south to begin my day and then re-trace my steps north. I may be sleeping in a lot of beds; however, I'm determined to hike every step past all the white blazes north.

With a portion of today's trail along the notorious roller coaster, a section with multiple ups and downs of varying lengths, I was beyond spent after a modest 13.5 miles. Even with my slackpack for the third consecutive day, my energy level plummeted before noon on day seventy-three. It took every ounce to make it back to the hostel by mid-afternoon. As I discussed with myself why I had felt so wasted for most of the day, I resolved to consume as many calories as I could before bedtime and to eat a larger breakfast the following morning.

Both of my tactics seemed to work. Throughout most of day seventy-four I hiked with renewed enthusiasm. The roller coaster continued; however, today I breezed through it without difficulty. Carrying a full pack, I hiked strong all day, arriving at the Appalachian Trail Conservancy in Harper's

Ferry, West Virginia shortly before it closed at 5:00 PM. The 19.8 miles had zipped by. Maybe it was the expectation of leaving Virginia, or maybe it was the increased caloric intake, or maybe it was wanting to arrive at the A.T. office before it closed. For whatever reason, when I signed in as thru-hiker number 318, and had my picture taken in front of the iconic building, I felt content.

Seventy-four days after leaving Springer Mountain I was at the psychological half-way point of my hike. The true half-way point awaited me a few days up the trail in Pennsylvania. For this moment, however, that fact was inconsequential. Everything just seemed more official now that I had reached Harper's Ferry.

After the brief visit at the conservancy I took a local shuttle bus to the nearby city of Charlestown, WV. Even though there were hostels in and nearby Harper's Ferry, I opted for a more comfortable room at a locally owned inn up the road a few miles. The decision proved fortuitous because a day later I would spot a familiar white Volvo station wagon in the parking lot of my motel. Perhaps it was fate, for after a planned day off, I would again be hiking with Molar Man.

Before continuing my hike with my old friend on day seventy-six, I used day seventy-five as a day of relaxation in Harper's Ferry. At least for most of the day I rested. To begin my day in the historic town, however, I decided to go ahead and hike the 0.6 miles from the trail leading to the Conservancy to High Street. This section of trail passes by iconoclastic Jefferson Rock. A photograph of the landmark has adorned the pages of many a history book.

When I arrived at High Street I strolled by a variety of shops and had lunch at a small tavern with Rock Steady, a thru-hiker I had met a couple of days earlier at Snickers Gap. Then I eventually caught the shuttle back to Charlestown. When I realized that Molar Man and Diane were at my motel, I arranged to join them for an early dinner.

Since I had last seen the couple in southern Virginia, Diane had also acquired a trail name, Sweet Tooth. She continued to offer support by arranging lunch deliveries to her husband, if a road near a trailhead were available.

And of course, she picked him up at the end of each day for a ride to a nearby motel or hostel.

As we dined I began to think about the possibility of partnering up with Molar Man again. Part of me wanted to continue solo while another reminded me that a guaranteed shuttle would make it easier for me to find a bed every night. Still as we parted ways after the meal, I had no intentions of pairing up with Molar Man for the duration of my hike. At least that was what I thought at the moment. Some things were about to change, however, as I got ready to enter my sixth state on the Appalachian Trail.

CHAPTER 7

Maryland and Molar Man

Some people stuck to the 15 miles a day like clockwork; others pushed big miles to get to town just to take a zero. I always admired how hard Don's Brother consistently pushed. I also know that was often due to the dangling 'carrot' or bed ahead. In fact, one of the things that will always stick with me about DB was his 'big miles and beds.'

Christopher "Grinch" Duda (Baton Rouge, LA)

AFTER THE DAY OF REST I took a taxi from Charlestown back to the A.T. at High Street. Since I wanted to get an early start, I opted for the more expensive ride over the shuttle bus. My initial destination for day seventy-six was a hostel at MD 17. This would have required a shuttle from an earlier road, probably US Alt 40. I could have then slackpacked a shorter 13.4 mile day and returned to the hostel for a second night.

My plan changed, however, when a steady rain began to fall in the early afternoon. Sweet Tooth was parked at Gathland State Park, dispensing snacks and soft drinks. So I broached the idea of hooking back up with the two at the end of my 17.5 mile day. Molar Man had started over seven miles behind me this morning and was planning to complete his day at Fox Gap and Reno Monument Rd. Sweet Tooth thought her husband would like my idea even though it meant an additional 1.1 miles.

I hiked through the constant, slightly cold rain, reaching Turners Gap a full hour before Molar Man was scheduled to arrive. After changing into some dry clothes I waited on the front steps of a church across the road. When my hiking buddy did reach the highway, I couldn't accurately ascertain whether he was irked over having to hike the added distance in a downpour or was rather pleased to have a partner once more. Either way, I was again on board, at least for a week, until Linda would be arriving to support me for a few days.

Since Molar Man had not had a day off in around two weeks, and since the following day's forecast called for heavy rain and thunderstorms, he wanted to zero. Even though I had just taken a day of rest in Harper's Ferry, I had no choice but to take another, that is if I wanted to join my buddy from our hiking days in Tennessee again. Their choice of destinations for the night was Hagerstown, MD, just off I-81.

With a supported hike, much reconnaissance work is needed to find roads in proximity to the trail. Although Sweet Tooth had a GPS, it always made her and Molar Man feel better if they scouted out their routes and meeting points in advance. On most days Molar Man had been starting his hikes at dawn and finishing by early or mid-afternoon. This method afforded them the opportunity to locate the next day or two's rendezvous points before dark.

On day seventy-seven the three of us drove to locations where Molar Man and I would be picked up after our hike the next three days. We also made a stop at Pine Grove Furnace State Park, the location of the Appalachian Trail Museum. Before leaving the park we visited the Pine Grove General Store. The business has been made famous by the A.T. thru-hiker half-gallon challenge. Since the park is just past the half-way point of the Appalachian Trail, many thru-hikers attempt to eat a half-gallon of ice cream in thirty minutes here. Relaxing on the patio, there were a few accepting the challenge on this lazy afternoon. Three days later Molar Man and I would choose to downsize our challenges to a half-pint of ice cream and a drumstick, respectively.

Day seventy-eight began before dawn. One thing that I quickly remembered about my days hiking with Molar Man in Tennessee was that he liked to get an early start. Still, I think I had forgotten just how early. After a 5:00 stop at McDonald's we took our first steps on the trail from Turners Gap at 5:45.

Hiking with a partner made the hours pass quickly. We covered the 23.5 miles in just over nine hours. With a good night's sleep in a bed, and the rather large fast food breakfast, the energy level remained high throughout the day. Most of today's terrain to Pen Mar Rd., and the Maryland-Pennsylvania border, could be called agreeable.

After another nourishing evening meal, a night in a bed, and a big breakfast, I experienced renewed fervor for my endeavor on day seventy-nine. Hiking at a steady pace throughout the morning, Molar Man and I knocked out 17.8 miles to US 30 near Fayetteville, PA, in less than seven hours. As it was in much of Pennsylvania, we were again in proximity to I-81. Finishing today's hike so early allowed my hiking buddy and Sweet Tooth time to scout out some more road crossings a little farther up the trail. The early conclusion also allowed me more time to rest in a room.

A few changes were on the horizon as day eighty dawned. With a 19.5 mile hike to PA 233 and Pine Grove Furnace State Park as our destination, Molar Man and I again started out early. Even though we hiked through a steady rain for much of the day, we reached a milestone at the physical half-way point of the trail. I didn't know it at the time, but I was also almost at the half-way mark of the number of days it would take me to complete the A.T.

The other change involved Linda, my wife. After today's hike, Molar Man and Sweet Tooth drove me to Carlisle, PA where I picked up a rental car. For the next five days my wife would be my shuttle driver. Initially, we were to be by ourselves for almost a week, but a delayed flight back in Georgia made it possible for me to continue on with Molar Man, at least for a few more days. This plan allowed Linda to follow Sweet Tooth in our car to the day's ending point. My somewhat direction-challenged spouse breathed a sigh of relief after finding out that she would not have to locate roads using a map and GPS. Following the navigation of Diane was much more to her liking.

After eighty days of thru-hiking the Appalachian Trail I had definitely embraced the philosophy of staying in towns and sleeping in beds whenever possible. I had hiked 1,115.2 miles past every white blaze, but was seldom spending a night in the woods. In fact, over those first eighty days, I had stayed at a motel 46 times, at hostels 13, and in shelters only 8. I had concluded my day at B & B's 5 times, in a tent just 3, at cabins 2, in a private home also 2, and even one night in a condo.

Many would-be thru-hikers begin their ventures with a goal to escape the conventions of (as thru-hiker Betterman called it) the "regular world." I had walked northward each day since March 23, on most days following the white blazes to a spot where the A.T. intersected with a road of some sort. From there I had on sixty-nine days been able to locate a bed or bunk. Sometimes I had hitched a ride. At others I had paid for a shuttle. Occasionally I had walked to a hostel or motel. And of course, I had been fortunate to be supported by Molar Man and Sweet Tooth for over a week.

So with a little less than half of my thru-hike remaining, I resolved to continue my method and seek out as many beds as I could find. The tactics were working well thus far. I saw no reason to alter my strategy now. I didn't know at the time; however, over the final eighty-four days on the trail, I would spend only six in shelters. There would be three nights in the ATC huts in the White Mountains, but all the rest would be in motels or hostels.

It didn't have an official name yet, but the soon to be called Don's Brother's Method was gaining a following. A few of my fellow thru-hikers shunned my strategy. Most, however, marveled at my ability to make my way to town so regularly. In fact, when I did spend an occasional, yet rare, night in the woods, those who knew of my tactics were often shocked when I claimed a spot in a shelter. I must admit that I felt for the young folks on a limited budget. I also was grateful for their companionship and acceptance, even if it was seldom that I joined them for a night in the wilderness.

CHAPTER 8

The Light Pack Prevails in Pennsylvania

Nearly anyone with average physical abilities can complete the AT. Yes, sprained ankles, twisted knees or occasional broken bones occur, but the physical requirements of hiking the trail are not the issue. Mental fatigue is. After the first few weeks, the euphoria of being free, climbing the mountains, being one with nature, etc. wears off. Then it becomes just one more day with four plus mountains to ascend and descend, another 15-20 miles to record in the books. The fact that, except for rhododendron in Georgia and Tennessee, all the states look similar adds to the tedium. Then, when the temperature rises and the mosquitoes arrive, 'torture' is a frequently heard comment. I found myself thinking often: I could be home sitting on the porch sipping a lemonade. Why am I putting myself through this? I could no longer think of just 700 miles to go. I had to resort to "I can make it through today. I'll see how tomorrow goes." Taking it one day at a time worked much better.

JOHN "MOLAR MAN" EICHELBERGER (SPRINGFIELD, OH)

WHEN I BEGAN MY HIKE of Pennsylvania with Molar Man two days earlier, I had no doubts that I could hike the entire 229 miles of the seventh state on the Appalachian Trail without spending a single night in the woods. On a section hike back in 2007, Alton and I had slackpacked the entire Keystone state.

During the first week Alton's wife, Susan, had served as our support person and picked us up from a road crossing at the end of each day.

After Susan flew back to Georgia we kept the car and shuttled each other. I would drop Alton at one trailhead each morning and then drive to where he planned to end the day's hike. This meant that I would have to hike in the opposite direction, so we would only see each other when we met on the trail. When he finished his hike he would drive back to get me. On some days we would alternate who dropped off whom. Even though this process can be time consuming, it's definitely one way to avoid nights in the woods.

And avoiding nights in the woods was what I was successfully doing. In order to continue hiking with Molar Man on day eighty-one, however, a 4:00 AM wake up was necessary. With Linda's flight delayed until the evening, I had called my buddy the night before to tell him the good (or bad, depending on how you look at it) news. Well before dawn I drove from Carlisle in my rental car to meet Molar Man and Diane at their motel off of PA 94. A short drive later we were back in Pine Grove Furnace State Park to continue the hike.

Across a few streams and over some rather large rocks, Molar Man and I made good time throughout the day, reaching Boiling Springs and the conclusion of a 19.6 mile hike by mid-afternoon. Sweet Tooth was waiting. Before departing the quaint, picturesque town, we visited the ATC Mid-Atlantic regional office, which is located right on the trail.

I concluded this eighty-first day of my thru-hike with a drive into Harrisburg to pick up Linda at the airport. Even though I was seldom sleeping on the A.T., it still seemed strange to be driving on an interstate highway and waiting in an airport terminal. When the flight did arrive, we stopped at a Cracker Barrel before heading to the motel in Carlisle. I had been sleeping in a lot of beds on this hike, but it was the first time I'd shared one since our last night in Dahlonega.

Day eighty-two began with introductions. Linda had heard all about Molar Man and Sweet Tooth from phone conversations, so meeting them in person was almost a little anti-climactic. Linda and Diane seemed to hit it off immediately. From Boiling Springs Molar Man and I hiked through rich farmland, quickly covering 10.2 miles to a road near the Conodoguinet Creek. The two ladies were parked with lunch at the Scott Farm Trail Work Center.

After a leisurely break with our wives, my hiking partner and I concluded our 16.5 mile day at PA 850. From there it was back to the cars for the drive to the motel. While many of our thru-hiking companions were dining on Ramen before curling up in their sleeping bags for the night, the four of us shared a nice dinner in Carlisle. The DBM isn't for everyone, but I never met a thru-hiker who turned down a restaurant meal.

Even though Molar Man and I didn't begin day eighty-three until 7:00, we found ourselves walking through historic Duncannon before 11:00. The famous (or maybe it should be infamous) Doyle Hotel wasn't even open yet. After passing through one of the most notorious towns on the entire A.T., we met the wives in a parking lot at the north end of the Clarks Ferry Bridge, US 22/322, by the Susquehanna River.

Also parked in the lot was Spirit, a lady who was supporting her thru-hiking husband, Steady. Spirit periodically meets her hubby at pre-determined spots along the A.T. in a small RV. Sweet Tooth had already met the Oregonian earlier on the trail. The kind-hearted Spirit invited Linda and me into the RV to enjoy our lunches.

This was A.T. hiking at its best, as far as I was concerned. I was walking with a light pack, having lunch delivered to me at a road crossing by my wife, and about to conclude the day's hike with a drive back to a town and a motel. The rocky trail in Pennsylvania was still challenging; however, with good food and a bed in which to sleep, the state that is cursed by many was becoming my favorite.

Still hiking with light packs for the sixth consecutive day, Molar Man and I began my day eighty-four with the ambitious goal of covering 25.6 miles. This would come within 0.1 of a mile of equaling my longest day so far. It would also prove to be the last 25-plus mile day of my hike.

With only one convenient road to meet Linda and Diane, we had no other choice but to have an early lunch with the ladies at PA 325. When we arrived at the site Pilgrim leaned against the Volvo. Apparently trying to persuade Sweet Tooth to drive him into a nearby town to pick up a package, Pilgrim looked tired. Diane graciously agreed to help. On that day in Pennsylvania Pilgrim got his first ride in the white Volvo. The next would come over seven hundred miles farther up the trail near the end of New Hampshire.

After the short respite, we continued to hike at nearly a 3 mile-per-hour pace throughout the remainder of the day. Having begun before 6:00 this morning, we reached the end of the day's walk slightly after 4:00. Since I had hoped to cover a marathon distance or beyond at least one time on my thru-hike, this would have been the perfect opportunity. Only 1.4 miles were needed to reach Swatara Gap and PA 72, but Molar Man did not want to alter the schedule. With almost 1000 miles yet to be hiked, I figured I'd eventually manage a 26.2 or beyond day. I never did and always regretted not walking on that day to Swatara Gap.

Day eighty-five would be the last that Molar Man and I would hike together in Pennsylvania. We didn't know if our paths would cross again somewhere farther north, but we thought they would. For the moment, however, my plans differed from his. Since the following day would be Linda's last before returning to Georgia, I wanted to spend some time with her. Therefore, I ended my day after a 12.8 morning while Molar Man continued on to total a 22.1 mile day.

This second stretch with Molar Man had been an extremely productive one. Over the past eight days, we had hiked 152.8 miles in Maryland and Pennsylvania. Granted, we were carrying light packs, being met with calorie-filled lunches and sleeping in beds every night. And yes, portions of the farmland of southern Pennsylvania are some of the least demanding miles of the entire trail. Only occasional rocky sections necessitated our hiking with diligence.

Still, we were 66 and 62 years old respectively and had hiked just a few miles shy of 1,200 since leaving Springer. Some of the young kids (I labeled anyone in their 20s this way) were hammering out big miles with full packs. But we old retired guys were just trying to make it to Maine the best way we knew how. For me that was as often as I could with a "light pack, big miles, and beds."

On the morning of day eighty-six I awoke in a motel room, anticipating my first day off since Maryland. The day dawned somewhat bittersweet. Linda would be headed to the Harrisburg airport and her return home. I would be left alone to enjoy the US Open Golf Tournament on TV. And it was Father's Day.

Knowing that I would be travelling without support, and, in all likelihood, carrying a full pack for the next few days at least, didn't really bother me. To be honest I was actually looking forward to hiking solo. Molar Man had been a good companion for the past eight days. Now, I wanted to hike at my pace and make all my own decisions again, for the time being anyway.

After telling Linda goodbye shortly before lunch, I perused the old *A.T. Guide* to determine the next day's destination. Since I wanted to stay a night in Hamburg, there appeared to be two sensible options. One was to make the walk there a two day undertaking with a night in a shelter. The other would require a 24.1 mile day with a full pack. Plus, the days were getting warmer.

So on the morning of day eighty-seven, I found myself doing something which I hadn't had to do since Harper's Ferry: pay for a shuttle. After arriving back at the trail off of PA 501, I still wasn't sure about my plan for the day. I just hiked. At times the trail afforded me the ability to cover more than three miles an hour.

Hiking at a steady pace, I arrived at the Eagles Nest Shelter after 15.1 miles by early afternoon. I quickly determined that there was no way that I was going to end my hike there with so much daylight remaining. Checking *The A.T. Guide*, I noted a Wendy's, Burger King, and Cracker Barrel near the Microtel in Hamburg. These were just too enticing to consider the shelter.

Even with the heat, and almost running out of water, I reached the outskirts of Port Clinton by late afternoon. Walking over the bridge, I gave myself a figurative pat on the back for managing the 24.1 miles solo with a full pack. It had been a lonely trail today, but I liked it. For the duration of the day I had seen only two others. Both were section-hikers.

Port Clinton offers a hotel and a B & B, but I had my sights set on the Microtel in Hamburg. Upon reaching the road, PA 61, I didn't even have time to remove my pack before a car stopped to offer a ride. The older couple was also shuttling another thru-hiker to town. I had intended to hitch, but this complimentary ride appeared before I had gotten my thumb out.

After I checked in at the Microtel I ventured up the street to Wendy's for supper. Several fast food restaurants, a Walmart, and a Cabela's are located near an I-78 exit. In the midst of so many luxuries, and being several days ahead of schedule, I decided to take an additional day off in Hamburg.

The following morning, day eighty-eight, I met fellow thru-hikers Medicine Man and Kudo in the breakfast area of the motel. I also chatted with a couple of section-hikers. I then just relaxed for most of the day before moseying over to Cracker Barrel. After a vegetable supper I headed back to the motel to plan the remainder of my hike through Pennsylvania. Beginning tomorrow, the state known for its rocks will become much more challenging. With another good night's sleep in a bed, I hoped I would be up for the task.

CHAPTER 9

Rocks and Rooms in Northern PA

DB's method of hiking is a great one for those who aren't crazy about sleeping outdoors. I grew up camping and have always enjoyed the social aspects of it and found that on the A.T., the time around the campsite was usually my favorite time of day. I did, however, thoroughly enjoy a hot shower, comfortable bed, and hearty meal every now and then. I suppose I can see why if you don't enjoy sleeping in the woods, the Don's Brother Method would be the perfect way to hike the A.T., or any trail for that matter.

RENEA "SPECK" WOODARD (LOGANVILLE, GA)

MY HIKE TOOK AN UNUSUAL turn on day eighty-nine. Like two days earlier when leaving Pine Grove, I wasn't exactly sure where I would lay my head at the end of the day. One option was to hike 26.3 miles with a full pack to PA 309 and the Blue Mountain Summit B & B. According to my memory, the rates there were high and the space was limited. In fact, on my section hike of PA, I had slept on a sofa in a seldom used portion of its restaurant.

Uncertain of my exact plans, I felt the day was off to a good start when I was able to hitch a ride with two men in a work truck. Fortunately they were leaving the motel about the same time that I was and also were headed to Port Clinton. The driver asked about my journey as we traversed the short 2.4 miles up PA 61. I gladly shared a few details and a quick story about Don.

Shortly after today's hike commenced, I found myself re-united with Speck, the section hiker from Georgia that I had first met north of Pearisburg. On the A.T. for another section-hike, Speck seemed happy to see me again. For much of the day we shared stories. Hers centered on the remainder of her trek through central Virginia. I, in turn, related some of my Molar Man tales. Speck hopes to reach somewhere in southern New Jersey this time out. As the day progressed it appeared that I'd found another hiking partner, at least for a week or so.

The one aspect of hiking the Appalachian Trail that Speck and I disagreed on was camping. She carried a stove and loved to sleep in the woods. Enjoying my fellow Georgian's company, I agreed to stopping at the Allentown Hiking Club Shelter after a 22.2 mile hike on a rather warm day. Really, it seemed the only logical decision since it was already after 6:00 when the shelter came into sight. With a full pack, I had tuckered myself out. Walking an additional 4.1 miles as darkness approached would have been foolish.

After 15 consecutive nights in a motel and 21 in either a bed or a bunk, I settled into a fairly nice shelter. Fortunately, I remembered how to blow up my Big Agnes sleeping pad. I hadn't utilized either the mattress or my sleeping bag since my second day in the Shenandoahs over three weeks earlier. I doubted that my 21 night streak in beds or bunks was a record, but I found it rather impressive. Not in any way trying to sound arrogant, but I was proud that my method of hiking the Appalachian Trail was working so beautifully.

The second day with Speck brought with it an array of challenging obstacles. Some were downright dangerous. First we were confronted with the knife edge. After painstakingly making our way along the narrow, sometimes jutted rocks of this somewhat infamous monolith, we were almost immediately faced with Bear Rocks. Bake Oven Knob followed a few miles later. This section of trail required patient, focused hiking, or should I say, rock climbing. Nevertheless, we navigated one of the most difficult sections I had encountered thus far without any mishaps. My hiking companion smiled often; I in turn grimaced with just a tad of fear.

Speck preferred sleeping in the woods, but if a hostel were available, she wasn't opposed. On this, my ninetieth day on the trail, Speck and I hiked 17.3

miles together, arriving at PA 873 near Palmerton by late afternoon. Within a few minutes we were able to hitch a ride into town. For A.T. hikers, Palmerton is known for the one-of-a-kind Jailhouse Hostel. Speck and I checked in and were greeted by several other thru-hikers that we had previously met. Two of these were father and son, Medicine Man and Kudo. We would hike with or around the duo until Speck's last day on the trail.

Knowing that the following day would be difficult, and wanting to hike over 20 miles, Speck proposed a slackpack day. So Speck called a lady listed in *The A.T. Guide* and asked if she would be willing to shuttle our gear to Wind Gap. Kathy agreed to pick up our gear in Palmerton in the morning and then meet us at the trailhead at PA 33 later that afternoon. This would be my first day with a light pack since leaving Molar Man.

Yesterday's hike posed some challenges. My day ninety-one began with a portion that I'd call treacherous. Many consider the climb out of Lehigh Gap one of the most difficult south of New Hampshire. In many ways it emulates the technical scrambles in the White Mountains. Having hiked a minuscule section of trail in the Whites, I agreed. Remembering when I had covered this ascent on my section-hike with Alton, I had almost dreaded this second time around. With Speck's company, however, the hike seemed more exhilarating than dangerous. The adrenaline accelerated all the way to the top. We exchanged satisfied smiles at the peak.

When Speck and I arrived at Wind Gap after a 20.8 mile day, we both were tired. I was certainly grateful that she had arranged the slackpack and the shuttle. Speck wanted to stay a night at Kathy's Victorian home B & B. I, however, was ready for a Quality Inn in East Stroudsburg and a steak dinner. After a hot shower, I walked to a restaurant meal before ending an exhausting day in a comfortable bed with my head on a soft pillow. Life was undoubtedly good "just a few miles off" the Appalachian Trail.

Since we only had a 15.7 day planned on my day ninety-two, Speck and I decided to take a later start. The shuttler first picked me up at my motel before stopping for Speck at her friend's. Then it was back to the trail at Wind Gap. With a town breakfast under my belt, and a sub sandwich in my light pack for lunch, I stepped back on the A.T. for my last day in Pennsylvania.

The day passed rather quickly with no significant obstacles until we reached the slightly technical Wolf Rocks. The fear I occasionally experienced yesterday seemed to have subsided. Maybe it was because of the company, but I was beginning to enjoy some of the rocks. Knowing that there were many more difficult sections between here and Katahdin, I figured the practice would come in handy.

Just before reaching the Delaware Water Gap, Speck found a desirable campsite. Before walking on to PA 611, I arranged a time to meet her the following morning. When I did arrive at the Gap, I phoned a lady whose number had been left along with some trail magic a few miles back up the trail. Trail angel Dolores happily drove me back to East Stroudsburg and another motel. I was very content not to be sleeping in the woods.

Like pretty much all of my nights in towns, my routine was to seek out a good restaurant within walking distance. After lingering at my table for almost two hours, I returned to my room and another good night's rest. Since Dolores had offered to drive me back to the A.T. the following morning, I would again be able to slackpack a 17.7 mile day. Before turning in for the night, I also called a local shuttle driver, Bob, to schedule a pick-up and return to East Stroudsburg at the end of tomorrow's hike.

Day ninety-three saw me re-uniting with Speck at the Delaware River Bridge. The New Jersey trail continued rocky in spots, but overall the terrain proved agreeable. We hiked a few miles with Steady whom we encountered near his and Spirit's RV in a parking lot on the New Jersey side of the river. We even saw Pilgrim again near a road crossing leading to the Mohican Outdoor Center.

Bob drove up a few minutes after Speck and I reached Blue Mountain Lakes Road. Rather than camping again, Speck decided to share my shuttle back to East Stroudsburg and get a room of her own for the night. We also made arrangements for Bob to drive us back to the trail the following morning.

CHAPTER 10

Roads and Delis in New Jersey and New York

As I went further north on the AT, I kept getting bummed about all the bad weather and mosquitoes. I was trying to keep my budget somewhat reasonable about staying in motels and hostels. At one point, I wrote this in one of the shelter journals: 'Tired of the rain and bugs. I'm headed to town to get a room and spend some of my grandkids' inheritance.' In total, I wound up spending 36 nights in hostels and 27 in motels. My record was 4 nights in a row in PA.

CARL "Z-MAN" ZIMMERMAN (AUSTIN, TX)

FOR THE PAST TWO DAYS I had taken a sandwich from town back to the trail for lunch. On day ninety-four, however, that wasn't necessary. I had been anticipating this day for a while, remembering that there were three places to get lunch only a few yards off the trail at US 206, Culvers Gap. When we arrived there, the steakhouse was closed. But fortunately, Gyp's Tavern wasn't. Medicine Man and Kudo joined Speck and me for lunch. I also purchased a sandwich for supper, knowing that I would be spending the night in the woods.

When we reached the Gren Anderson shelter after a 13.6 mile day, others were already gathered around a picnic table adjacent to the structure. Thru-hiker Pfeiffer almost swooned in disbelief when she discovered that I was sleeping on the trail.

"I can't believe you're not going to the next town," the saucy lass stated sarcastically. "Do you really think you can survive in the woods for a night?"

Come to think of it, she had a point. I could have hiked an additional six miles to the Deckertown Turnpike and hitched a ride from a parking area there to Port Jervis, NY. Or for that matter, I could have continued on to NJ 23, another 5.3 miles, from where I could have called a taxi. But since Speck and I had walked at a leisurely pace throughout the day, and stopped for a lengthy lunch, it was now too late to continue.

"Every now and then, you just have to rough it," I replied to Pfeiffer.

She and her hiking companion, Lentil, actually seemed impressed with the number of nights I had spent in a town. Like many other thru-hikers, Pfeiffer certainly was aware of my method. We had been hiking in proximity to each other since central Virginia. Even though she camped most of the time, she too enjoyed a night in a motel. In fact, the first time we met was at the Howard Johnson's in Daleville. As I reminded her, there were dozens of thru-hikers in rooms on that occasion.

Those who knew me well also knew my propensity for bringing town food back to the trail. As Pfeiffer, Lentil, Speck, and "older than me" Pilgrim cooked supper over tiny stoves, I pulled out my turkey sandwich which I'd purchased earlier in the day at Gyp's. I also had a bag of chips and a coke to go along with it. Even though soft drinks would be far from cold, they still made the dining experience in the woods more tolerable. I drank water and Gatorade during the day, but almost always carried a soda to enjoy with my meals.

When I finished my supper I prepared my mat and bag in the cramped conditions. The unwelcome mosquitoes, that had been pestering all of us for hours, buzzed around my head as I closed my eyes. I even slept in my one long-sleeved shirt in an attempt to keep the pests from attacking. Spraying the shirt with insect repellent didn't really matter since I knew that I would be able to do laundry the next day. A hot shower and a bed were also on the morrow's agenda.

Surprisingly, I felt rather refreshed on the morning of day ninety-five, after an unexpected good night's sleep in the capacity-filled shelter. Today's hike would be a short one. With plans to travel to New York City tomorrow,

I only needed to get to NJ 23, an 11.3 mile walk. This would also be Speck's last day on the trail.

Other than the constant attacks from the merciless mosquitoes, I enjoyed the last day with my hiking partner. By early afternoon we reached the High Point State Park Headquarters at NJ 23. Bob, a section hiker who had also stayed in the shelter the previous night, provided a ride to a motel a couple of miles from Port Jervis, NY. After checking into my room I later met Speck, Medicine Man and Kudo in the on-site restaurant. The father and son had decided to end their thru-hike attempt, so we all made plans to take the Metro North/New Jersey Transit into New York the following morning.

There are several locations near the trail that provide a Metro North rail line into the city. I had used the train to get from NYC to the A.T. on my section hike of Connecticut and Massachusetts, and also used it to get back to the city at the conclusion of my New Jersey/New York section hike. Both times I was flying to or from LaGuardia.

Since day ninety-six would be another rest day, I decided to keep my room in Port Jervis for a second night. This is not a town that many Appalachian Trail hikers frequent; however, I found it to have much to offer. In addition to the easily accessible train station and a moderately priced diner, the taxi fare was the cheapest I had found anywhere along the trail. Each time I used a cab the charge was $5.00, except the shuttle back to the trail at High Point State Park, which was $15.00.

So after an early morning Burger King breakfast, Speck, Medicine Man, Kudo and I boarded the train before 8:00. I wouldn't be on the trail on day ninety-six, but it would be one of the most memorable of the entire journey. I would spend about two hours with my daughter, Rachel, who lives and works in Manhattan. When I compiled a list of all the places I had had a meal on my 2013 thru-hike, New York City was among them.

After my brief visit with Rachel came to an end, I had to wait a couple of hours at the Secaucus Junction station for the commuter train back to Port Jervis. When I did finally get back I grabbed another fast food meal before returning to my motel and another good night's sleep in a bed. I also made arrangements for a shuttle back to the A.T. the following morning.

A congenial taxi driver dropped me back at High Point State Park early on day ninety-seven. For the first time in over a week, I found myself hiking solo again. With Speck back home in Georgia and Molar Man somewhere up the trail, I felt a little lonely. Fortunately the 20.6 mile hike went rather rapidly even though I took my worst fall of the entire hike about four miles south of my destination for the day, Vernon, NJ. The full pack actually helped prevent me from what could have been a serious injury when I landed on my back.

Having already hiked this section of trail eight years earlier, I was also aware of the numerous spots to get meals. New Jersey and New York are sometimes referred to as the "deli states." This part of the trail definitely fit the Don's Brother Method. Hikers who have the money and don't mind walking off trail a short distance can enjoy a meal just about every day. Today I stopped for a turkey sandwich, chips, and a Dr. Pepper at Horler's Store, about half a mile up Lott Rd. Rather than trying to hitch, I just walked into Unionville, New York. Even though I was hiking in New Jersey, the trail runs in close proximity to the state line.

Later in the afternoon I decided to partake of a second lunch at the Heaven Hill Farm, located where the trail intersects NJ 94 leading into Vernon. I bought a large barbecue sandwich and another soft drink at the combination farmer's market, deli, and nursery. After finishing my snack, I scored a free ride into town with the proprietor of the deli.

My destination for the evening was the hostel run by the St. Thomas Episcopal Church. Even though I had to sleep on my mat on the floor, at least I had a bathroom for a hot shower. Kitchen privileges are provided as well. Some cots were also available; however, all had been taken when I arrived. The old church hostel was teeming with thru-hikers at the end of a very hot day.

I awoke early on day ninety-eight. First I walked up the street about a hundred yards to the Mixing Bowl, a restaurant in a purple-painted old home. After enjoying a large country breakfast, I strolled back to the hostel to pack up. I was looking forward to entering my ninth state on today's hike.

A short while later I stood back at NJ 94 with my thumb out. I was quickly able to hitch a ride back to the trailhead. My destination for the day was Greenwood Lake, NY, and the Breezy Point Inn. I had called yesterday to ensure that I got one of the five rooms at the combination motel, restaurant, and bar.

When I reached NY 17A I first walked up the highway to the Creamery for a cold treat on the hot afternoon. After leisurely enjoying a root beer at the end of a 15.0 mile day, I engaged an elderly patron in conversation. Gene, who identified himself as a retired soldier, offered a ride into town. By using my "town to town" approach often, I continue to meet interesting locals.

The Breezy Point looked exactly as I remembered it. Alton and I had stayed a night here on the New Jersey/New York section hike of eight years earlier. Windows face directly toward the deck of the restaurant which overlooks Greenwood Lake. Later that evening I dined on seafood and listened to music, which continued late into the evening. It was almost a certainty that I was the only Appalachian Trail thru-hiker in town tonight. I still preferred the good food and a soft bed to tortillas and a shelter.

The following morning, day ninety-nine, found me again feasting on a large country breakfast, this time at Murphy's Bar and Grill. When I asked my waitress if there were a taxi service in town, the bartender overheard our conversation. Apparently wanting to do a little trail magic of his own, he called me a cab and even paid my fare. With over 800 miles left to be hiked, I was grateful for any opportunity to save a few dollars.

My original plan for the day was to hike either to the Fingerboard or William Brien Memorial Shelter. I had purchased some trail food for my night in the woods at a small market before leaving Greenwood Lake. Hiking without much enthusiasm throughout the morning, I decided to alter my itinerary. Since I was already planning to spend two nights in Fort Montgomery, NY, I started looking at options for making it three.

If I wanted to continue sleeping in beds, I'd have to use a shuttle from one of two roads that intersected with the A.T. In hindsight it might have been an easier commute from the other end of Arden Valley Rd., an additional 5.9 miles farther up the trail. But the wiser choice wasn't always the one selected.

So with a new plan in mind, I chose to stop after a 12.0 mile day at NY 17. From there I would shuttle into Fort Montgomery and use the Bear

Mountain Bridge Motel as a base from which to slackpack a couple of days. Not wanting to risk failing to get a hitch from a somewhat isolated road crossing, I called the number of a car service. This was one of several times I relied on the A.T. Conservancy site for a list of shuttle services. Knowing that the Bear Mountain Bridge Motel only had six rooms, I also called ahead to get a reservation. This was another place I had stayed back in 2005.

Before I arrived at the highway, Doug, a former US Army soldier, called to make sure I was still planning to stay at his motel since all rooms were booked. I assured him I was. I suppose he feared that a room might go unused because he called again a short while later.

After waiting for over an hour, I was beginning to think that I might be stranded. Finally the driver arrived and I was off to another night in a bed. Even though this strategy worked for me, it was pricey since I also had to use the same service to return to the trail. For the time being, however, I was back in a room and only about a tenth of a mile from a barbecue restaurant. It would be where I dined for the next three nights.

With a slackpack and a bed to return to, I again hiked enthusiastically all 19.8 miles of my 100th day on the trail. The sandwich I had purchased at a bagel shop before leaving Fort Montgomery made for a tasty lunch. And as always, I carried a soft drink with which to enjoy it. At the hike's conclusion, I was picked up by Doug, who, along with his wife Ingrid, owns the Bear Mountain Bridge Motel.

I started day 101 with a bagel sandwich from the shop across the street before again being transported back to the trail by Doug. Today's hike began with a walk over the Bear Mountain Bridge which spans the Hudson River. Visibility was limited on the foggy morning. Eventually the fog turned to a light rain, and within minutes it was flooding. Fortunately, I was almost to the Appalachian Market where the trail crosses US 9 to Peekskill when the deluge commenced.

I again saw the need to make some adjustments. Rather than hike through the predicted storms, I opted to return to my comfortable motel room after a short 5.8 mile day. The first person I asked inside the market, a NYC fireman, provided the ride. I gratefully thanked the public servant who had deviated from his normal route to get this very wet hiker back to town. While many thru-hikers invariably continued on under the adverse conditions, I felt very blessed to be utilizing my strategy of finding beds whenever they were available.

Since I had to get back to the A.T. crossing at US 9, my best option was the car service. When the route back to the trail involves more than one highway, hitches are more difficult. It was also with a full pack that I reluctantly vacated the cozy room I had occupied for the past three nights.

As I headed up the trail on day 102, I was aware that there were multiple opportunities to find another room over this stretch. I could probably easily have hitched into Poughquag or Pawling and set up another base. However, the shuttle from Dennytown Rd. or NY 301 would have been lengthy. Plus, I had plans to meet one of my friends from home the following day. Good running buddy John Teeples wanted to experience a few days of trail life.

So because I was packing town food for lunch, and because I knew that town food was available for supper, I arrived at the decision to stop for the night at the RPH shelter, a block structure which contains bunk space for six. Since the shelter sits a stone's throw from Hortontown Rd., it's a popular spot for ordering pizza. The six other thru-hikers present and I all chose to honor the tradition.

It felt good being in the company of these young folks, most of whom I had seen on the trail over the past several days. Sleeping intermittently due to the mosquitoes, I took solace knowing that there were still many beds awaiting me between this shelter and Katahdin. I didn't know it on this stifling evening, but this would be the final night I would sleep in the woods until New Hampshire. I was about to spend the next 27 nights of my Appalachian Trail thru-hike in a bed or a bunk. The time had arrived to get serious with my "light pack, big miles, and beds" philosophy.

Cold leftover pizza has never been my breakfast of choice. However, since there were several slices remaining, I managed to stuff down a couple. Knowing that I could stop for another meal later on the morning of day 103, I doubted that my energy levels would get low.

At NY 52 to Stormville, I strolled up the road the 0.4 of a mile to the Mountaintop Market Deli. I selected a breakfast sandwich from the menu and ordered two chocolate milks to accompany it. Then I got a free ride back to the trail from a local man who liked helping hikers.

When I reached NY 55 after a 12.3 mile day, I hitched a ride to the Duches Motor Inn near Wingdale. After checking in, showering, and arranging for my clothes to be laundered, I walked just up the road a piece to yet another barbecue restaurant. Being from the south, I'm always interested in how these northern establishments compare. Big W's met all the expectations of this southern man. My only regret was not getting some take-out for later in the evening. When John arrived shortly before midnight, he would have certainly appreciated it. With a complicated travel schedule, he had missed supper. It would be the following morning at a small grocery store before he would get a good meal.

CHAPTER 11

Towns in Connecticut

After experiencing the DBM or Don's Brother's Method of hiking, I am convinced that it's the only way to enjoy the beauty of the trail without those pesky, negative pack and bed adjectives—you know: heavy pack, wet pack, hard bed, wet bed—no encumbrances in the woods means greater enjoyment of and appreciation for God's creation and fellow travelers!

JIMMY BROOKS (COLUMBUS, GA)

ON MY 104TH DAY ON the Appalachian Trail I again had a hiking partner, at least for the next three days. John and I took a taxi back to the trail at NY 55 where I had concluded yesterday. My original idea was to stop at Ten Mile River Shelter so that John could experience a night in the woods. Somewhere in the afternoon, however, the plan changed. Even though he had all the necessary backpacking gear, John let me know early in the day that he would be more than happy to use the Don's Brother Method. After passing the river, we walked an additional 1.5 miles to Bulls Bridge Rd. to conclude an 18.8 mile day.

We chose to call a taxi rather than trying to hitch. From the intersection of the A.T. with the road, we were driven first to Cornwall Bridge, Connecticut. When we discovered that there really weren't any restaurants in the area, John and I both agreed that Kent, Connecticut was a better choice. A phone call later, we had reservations at the Cooper Creek B & B. Before going there, however, we stopped in Kent for a large Italian meal.

Sweaty and dirty from the hot day on the trail, John and I changed shirts in the parking lot and then spruced up a bit in the restroom before following our hostess to a table. After consuming around two thousand calories to replenish our losses for the day, we called Cooper for a ride to his inn.

The room fell short of the 2 and 3 star motels I preferred; however, it did have two beds. The only upstairs bath was located in the hall. Since we were the sole patrons, we didn't have to share.

After the fairly long day and carrying my full pack, I felt exhausted. Finding it difficult to muster enough mental energy to write, I chose first to nap for an hour. Conversation awakened me before my watch alarm. In somewhat of a dreamlike state, after the brief rest, I realized that the person talking with John was another friend from back home, Jimmy Brooks. John knew of Jimmy's plans. I didn't. There weren't many times during the entire thru-hike that I remembered feeling this content. My good buddies would be joining me for two more days.

On the morning of day 105, John, Jimmy, and I enjoyed a hearty breakfast prepared by Cooper's wife, Mary. Jimmy had even brought some instant grits after reading how much I was missing them with my country breakfasts. They made the scrambled eggs, sausage, toast, and coffee even that much tastier. The meal satisfied my nutritional needs for the morning of a planned 18.3 mile day.

As I have stated before, a thru-hike doesn't have to be drudgery, if the hiker is able to and doesn't mind spending some money. Because I was eating and sleeping well, I was hiking stronger and "most" of the time enjoying the adventure. Many would not embrace the Don's Brother Method, but it was definitely working for me.

Another surprise that my new companions proposed was utilizing one pack containing only food, water, and a first aid kit. Since the three of us would be returning to the Cooper Creek B & B for a second night, John's idea made good sense. The two also insisted that they alternate carrying the gear, which allowed me to hike packless for the day. Even though I offered to take a turn, my friends refused my request. I appreciated their generosity on another hot, buggy day.

When the three of us reached CT 4, near Cornwall Bridge, Connecticut, Cooper was waiting for the ride back to his home. After giving us time for hot showers, he also drove us to Kent so that we could again dine substantially. With the abundance of pasta I was consuming, I briefly feared that I might be the only 2013 thru-hiker to actually gain weight. Still I treated myself to a snack later that evening before hitting the sack.

Day 106 would in many ways mirror the previous. Cooper shuttled my two buddies and me back to CT 4 after Mary's pancake breakfast. He also agreed to transport most of our gear to where he would meet us in the afternoon. So like yesterday, Jimmy and John took turns shouldering the one pack. I was again grateful, especially when we arrived at St. John's Ledges. This steep, 500 foot descent over one mile had caused some trepidation back in '04. Today, however, I managed the section flawlessly. John and Jimmy had hoped for more of a challenge.

Having companions with whom to hike enhanced my day. Still, I felt a tad of sadness, knowing that it would be the final one that my friends from home would be joining me. The Toymakers Café, about a quarter mile off the trail in Falls Village, Connecticut, seemed an appropriate site to end today's hike and our time together. After all, this spot also afforded the three of us one final opportunity to share a meal. Hot lunches in proximity to the Appalachian Trail were always special. This one was even more so because I was enjoying it with my pals.

After a leisurely time of fellowship, John, Jimmy and I parted ways. Cooper arrived to transport them to a Metro-North train station for a commute to New York City and eventually to LaGuardia and a flight back to Georgia. As for me, I needed to find another bed for the night. There was no doubt where that was going to be, that is if she had space available.

Before leaving Falls Village I placed a call to Maria McCabe, somewhat of an A.T. legend who rents rooms in her home in Salisbury. The feisty, eighty-something year-old, great-grandmother agreed to pick me up on the western side of the Housatonic River. She first informed me that the bridge into Falls

Village was closed to vehicular traffic. I concluded a 14.0 mile day under a shade tree, awaiting Maria's arrival.

Having stayed a night with the kind-hearted woman on my Connecticut-Massachusetts section hike, I knew of her "hiker's package." A clean room, ride to and from the laundry, kitchen privileges, and first rate hospitality are included.

When I reminded Maria that I had spent a night in her home back in 2004, she replied, "I barely remember last week." I enjoyed the fine lady's company, and the cold drink she had brought me, on the ride back to Salisbury.

The room she assigned me upstairs happened to be the same I had shared with Alton nine years earlier. I had it to myself even though there were twin beds. When I told Maria that I'd like to stay two nights, she said she would have to move me to the "big" room the following night. It contained a full size bed, an air-conditioner, and a TV. She expected a full house the next day.

As I began to unpack, I heard a familiar voice from the small room at the end of the hall.

"I can't believe I'm running into you again," the white-haired Pilgrim said with a smile. It was the first time I had seen my California friend since the Gren Anderson shelter in New Jersey.

"I see you're still sleeping in beds whenever you get the chance," Pilgrim stated.

"It looks like you're in one too," I replied.

We both laughed. I was quick to remind my fellow sojourner that we had first met at a hostel in Virginia, and then later at another a little farther up the trail. After we picked at each other for a few minutes, Pilgrim gladly accepted my supper invitation. Even though I had lost my hiking partners from the past few days, at least I wouldn't be eating alone tonight.

Salisbury offers several dining choices in various price ranges. We kind of splurged, selecting the slightly upscale Country Bistro. Over dinner Pilgrim and I shared stories about our previous few weeks on the A.T. He still looked dangerously underweight. Somewhat concerned himself, Pilgrim noted that he needed to eliminate some more gear. I recommended my way of hiking.

Although wanting to continue a more traditional hike, spending the majority of his nights in the woods, Pilgrim realized that my method made sense for him. For the moment, however, he wasn't ready to make the change.

Later in the evening, while examining *The A.T. Guide*, I noticed how I could use Salisbury as a base for three nights and still hike every day. When I approached Maria with the idea, she hesitatingly agreed to provide a shuttle. She added that she would have to assess a fee determined by mileage. That sounded fair to me.

As day 106 came to a close, I lay in a bed with my head on a soft pillow. An oscillating fan provided comfort on a very warm night. And I again felt relieved that it looked like I could avoid sleeping in the woods for a while longer. The trail crossed roads often in Connecticut and Massachusetts. Roads led to towns with motels and restaurants. My plan was to continue sleeping and eating well, at least until Vermont.

Maria couldn't drive me back to the trail near Falls Village until 9:00 the following day. Since I only had a short 8.3 mile hike scheduled, I had time for breakfast in town. Maria's home is located about three-hundred yards from the center of Salisbury. On a sleepy Sunday morning, I had to wait until 8:00 before the bistro opened.

After enjoying my bacon and eggs, I took my third cup of coffee out to the patio and joined Colin. The ex-Marine from Pennsylvania had just walked into Salisbury and planned to head back to the trail after his meal. It's not like I'm the only Appalachian Trail thru-hiker who eats town food. It's just that I do it more often.

On the ride back to Housatonic River Road, I broached the question with Maria about shuttling me the following day as well. The elderly lady wasn't doing many shuttles these days, so she was somewhat apprehensive. I assured her that I would plan to get to the highway before her arrival so that it would be I, not she, who had to wait.

"I'll have to charge you for a ride that far."

"That's fine, Maria. I'll pay you whatever you think is fair."

"And you'll need a ride back to the trail the next day too. You'll have to pay me for gas again for that ride."

"That's OK. I'd be grateful." The final seven miles of a northbound hike through Connecticut are among the most difficult in the state. Plus the first eleven miles of Massachusetts are equally as challenging. An opportunity to slackpack the Taconic Range would definitely be welcomed.

But before getting to the next day, I had to cover the "almost easy" miles from where I had left the trail yesterday near Falls Village to Undermountain Rd. There are actually three ways to get into Salisbury. The A.T. crosses at US 44, again at Cobble Road, and finally at Undermountain. I chose the latter because of the short distance of today's hike as well as because I wanted to keep my distance the following day manageable.

Day 107 ended with a little over a half-mile road walk back to Maria's home on Grove Street. With a full afternoon free, I lounged in the spacious backyard for a while. I wrote my journal entry for the day before walking back into Salisbury for another night of fine dining at the bistro. Three other thru-hikers were staying the night with Maria, but they all chose to eat at a pizzeria near the laundromat. It's rare not to see other hikers at a restaurant in a trail town. But that's the way it was at the Country Bistro on a Sunday evening.

Since I wouldn't need a shuttle to get back to the trail on day 108, I planned an early start. I awoke at 5:00 and prepared myself three eggs, toast, and juice for an adequate breakfast. Then I walked the half-mile or so road miles back to where I had left the A.T. yesterday. With what I knew would be an arduous day of hiking ahead of me, I took my first step on the trail at 6:10.

Despite some painstakingly slow descents, beauty appeared often in many fashions. From the crest of Bear Mountain to the rushing waters of Sages Ravine, nature's grandeur was continuously revealed. The most scenic views of the day were from Race Mountain. A 650 foot ascent of Mt. Everett followed. After reaching the other end of Everett, Jug End and another 1000 foot descent greeted me.

By the time I reached MA 41, ten hours and 17.8 miles later, I was beyond tired. It definitely felt good knowing that Maria would be arriving shortly to drive me back to her home for the night. With a hot shower, restaurant meal, and bed in my immediate future, I smiled, realizing that I had reached the tenth state on my journey to Maine.

I also noted that all my nights in Connecticut had been spent in only two places: the Cooper Creek B & B near Kent and Maria's home in Salisbury. The trail crosses roads often and there are plenty of places to lodge and eat. I would also recommend the Bearded Woods hostel, run by former thru-hiker, Hudson and his wife, Big Lu. Located near the trail in Sharon, CT, it's one of the nicest places I've stayed. Even though I chose to use Maria McCabe's while on this section of trail during my thru-hike, I spent a night at Bearded Woods on another A.T. venture in the summer of 2014. Hudson also offers shuttles to and from the trail at nearby road crossings.

CHAPTER 12

Motels of Massachusetts

It was around Front Royal that I first met Don's Brother. I was having trouble getting my weight back after two bouts with the Norovirus. After explaining his method of hiking I was intrigued with the idea of hiking highway to highway and really liked the idea of shedding the weight of my tent and three days of food. But I was a pretty stubborn guy and wanted to finish the trail the traditional way. As it turned out I called DB when I couldn't lift my pack anymore while in Great Barrington, MA. His method was a Godsend that helped me extend my trek through the Whites and into the beginning of Maine before my body gave out on me. I liked his method so well, that I forsook my tent and went with the DB method for all of Maine two years later when I went back to complete the Appalachian Trail.

I highly recommend the DB method. You still hike the trail albeit with a lighter pack, still meet and make friends with all its hikers, but you do it while eating a proper breakfast and dinner.

JOE "PILGRIM" ESTES (WEST HILLS, CA)

NOT ONLY WAS I ABOUT to hike my first full day in Massachusetts, but the hike as a whole was in for a major change. Even though my Georgia friends, John and Jimmy, had joined me briefly, I hadn't had a regular hiking partner since Speck departed. My last thru-hiker companion, Molar Man, and I had gone our separate ways in Central Pennsylvania. Perhaps it was fate or maybe someone was looking out for me, but through somewhat of a coincidence, I'd gain two hiking buddies on day 109.

The previous night I received a text message from Pilgrim indicating that he needed to change his tactics if his hike were going to continue. Still unable to gain weight, the 66 year-old was struggling. I was more than happy to invite the man I had first met over 500 trail miles earlier to join me for a while. Pilgrim was already near Great Barrington at the East Mountain Retreat Center. I suggested that he head on into town and get a room at the Travel Lodge. I would then hike the 12.0 miles to MA 23 and hitch a ride to meet him. Pilgrim liked the idea.

Maria couldn't return me to the trail at MA 41 until 9:00, so I again walked into Salisbury. My first stop was the Post Office. Since I had not been using my sleeping bag lately, and since my plan was to frequent motels and hostels exclusively throughout the remainder of Massachusetts and all of Vermont, I decided to ship the bag ahead. I smiled a little when sealing the box, knowing that the light pack would be even lighter.

Then I headed to a coffee shop for breakfast. Sitting at a table on the patio, my old friend Banzai greeted me. With a thick black beard and shaggy hair, Banzai looked haggard.

"May I join you," I asked before sitting down with my cup of coffee. "How's it going, good buddy?" I continued.

"This hike just isn't much fun anymore," Banzai remarked with an inkling of indifference. I agreed, noting that the bugs, especially the mosquitoes, had been relentless.

"Some people may say they're still having fun, but deep down, I think everyone is miserable," Banzai stated.

"I can't say that I disagree with you. I'm headed into Great Barrington tonight for a motel and then will join up with Pilgrim. He wants to try my method of staying in rooms, eating town food, and slackpacking. Why don't you come along with us? We can share shuttle expenses and a room occasionally."

Banzai looked interested. His countenance changed and the twinkle seemed to return to his blue eyes as he thought about my proposition. When I offered him a share of my shuttle at no cost, he was sold. Half an hour later we were both in Maria's small compact on our way back to the A.T.

Great Barrington, Massachusetts may be reached by either of two roads which intersect with the Appalachian Trail. The first is US 7. Banzai and I arrived at this crossing after only 3.6 miles, so I decided to continue to the second option at MA 23. Even though I had covered a mere 12.0 miles with minimal elevation changes, swarming mosquitoes kept me from enjoying any part of the hike. I just wanted to get into town and a room. Sure, I had been in a bed the past five nights in Connecticut, but each of them had been in someone's home. I wanted the seclusion and privacy of a motel room again.

Seeing a pick-up truck in the distance, I stuck out my thumb as I crossed MA 23, hoping for a quick hitch. To my surprise, the truck stopped. My good fortune continued with a ride into Great Barrington with Sub Zero, a section-hiker who lived in the area. Not only did he take me to the Travel Lodge, but he also agreed to pick up my buddies and me after the following day's hike. Sub Zero certainly met all the qualifications of a true trail angel.

When we talked by phone last night, Pilgrim had offered to share his room. I decided, however, to get my own, at least for the first night in town. Banzai opted for another, slightly less expensive motel. The plan was to meet for breakfast the following morning before heading back to the trail together.

I checked in, took a hot shower, and then met Pilgrim to discuss our itinerary for the next few days. He first wanted to go to the post office and mail some gear home. He also wanted to purchase some tennis shoes to use in towns. After the errands we strolled over to a nearby McDonald's for some fast food. Although not too nutritious, these rather fatty meals sustained me throughout much of my hike. When I returned to the regular world in September, I actually discovered that my cholesterol and triglycerides had both decreased. It had to have been the exercise.

So I concluded day 109 with a meal at McDonald's and began day 110 at the same establishment. The young lady who asked to take my breakfast order must have wondered about me as I stared at the overhead menu. I didn't reveal that I was trying to count calories to determine how many I thought I could consume. About 1200 looked reasonable.

After the meal Banzai, Pilgrim, and I walked a few blocks to the intersection of US 7 and MA 23. We had barely assumed a positon for hitching when a van pulled over. Banzai concluded that the almost immediate ride indicated that it was good luck to be hiking with Don's Brother. For me, it just felt comfortable knowing that I'd be sharing the trail and expenses with two fellow thru-hikers that I'd first met in Virginia. None of us knew how long we'd stay together; however, for at least the next few days, we had a plan. Of course both Banzai and Pilgrim had begun their thru-hikes on days different from mine. Therefore, the day numbers I will continue to state will only relate to my hike. Yes, day 110 denoted a new beginning.

In order to end the day's hike at a road crossing, we were only able to cover 12.2 miles to Main Rd., a little less than a mile east of Tyringham, MA. Yesterday's trail angel, Sub Zero, met us in his pick-up truck for the ride back to Great Barrington. The general contractor shared some information about the area and also talked a little about his own section-hiking of the A.T. Good folks just keep appearing to help this "old" hiker along the way.

Before heading back to the Travel Lodge, Sub Zero dropped Banzai at his motel. For the first time on my journey, I decided to share a room. Since it looked like I would have companions for the immediate future, it only made sense to occasionally cut my expenses. Previously I had occupied cabins, hostels, and shelters with other hikers; however, now I had the opportunity to reduce my motel bill by half. This would become a common experience over the next 500 miles. In fact, I may have been one of the few thru-hikers any year who had not at least roomed with another hiker once prior to arriving in Massachusetts.

After an always refreshing hot shower and a restful afternoon, I joined Pilgrim and Banzai at Ena, a Greek restaurant across the highway from the motel. It seemed to be an appropriate time to add yet another type of cuisine to this thru-hiker's resume. My buddies also appeared happy to be eating town food exclusively for a while. Hopefully, all this fine dining would put some much needed weight on Pilgrim. As for Banzai and me, we were just trying to maintain.

Over dinner the three of us mapped out our plans for the next few days. There was the option of a short 6.9 mile walk to Upper Goose Pond Cabin, which sounded like somewhat of a cross between a hostel and a shelter. Located about a half mile off the trail, it would have sufficed under other more traditional circumstances. However, after only a couple of days on what Banzai labeled the Don's Brother Method, my friends were already getting a little spoiled. They readily agreed to my suggestion.

I proposed that we hike the 18.0 miles from Main Rd. to Washington Mountain Rd. The A.T. crosses the road just a few yards from the home of Roy and Marilyn Wiley. Having used Roy for a shuttle on my section hike of this area, I knew that he provided rides into Pittsfield for a modest fee. A moderate-sized town, Pittsfield has a Quality Inn and a Friendly's. I offered the idea of calling Roy to see if he would pick up our gear in Great Barrington and have it for us at his home. These strategies would allow us to slackpack another day and have our gear and a shuttle waiting for us at the hike's conclusion. Banzai and Pilgrim marveled at my ingenuity. Both seemed pleased to be on board.

When I reached Roy by phone, he didn't seem as enthused with our plan as we did. Nevertheless, he agreed to be at the Travel Lodge at 7:00 the next morning. The soft-spoken gentleman found the DBM to be an intriguing method for navigating the Appalachian Trail. Roy didn't really ever acknowledge whether he approved or disapproved of our strategy. With all the hikers who have passed by, or tented in the yard of his home, he certainly must have many stories to tell. Perhaps we would become one of them.

Even though it had been nine years since I had last seen Roy Wiley, he looked about the same as I recalled. When he arrived at the Travel Lodge in Great Barrington for the shuttle back to the A.T., Roy displayed the same quiet, unassuming demeanor that I remembered. Although non-judgmental, Roy didn't appear to really embrace the Don's Brother Method like Banzai and Pilgrim when I explained it to him. But then he wasn't the one hiking. We were just grateful that Roy was willing to help us on this section of trail.

The Don's Brother Method

Day 111 proved to be a gold star day for the DBM. As always, I took fast food back to the trail for lunch when leaving a town. Today I had a couple of McDonald's hamburgers in my pack. Burgers that were cooked the night before aren't the tastiest treats for the noonday meal, but they sure beat trail food as far as I'm concerned. What made today's lunch different was a microwave.

The A.T. crosses US 20, 5.0 miles east of Lee, MA. A small "mom and pop" motel sits only about 0.1 mile east. Spotting a picnic table adjacent to the rural inn, my buddies and I decided to scout out the area. When I asked the proprietor if there were a coke machine we could use, he pointed toward a breakfast room off the tiny lobby. Not only were we going to have cold soft drinks with our lunch, but the burgers were going to be warm as well. We all smiled, seeing the microwave on the wooden table.

"I'm really liking the Don's Brother Method," Banzai remarked as his Coca-Cola was dispensed.

We all were. How could we complain about anything, even on another hot, buggy afternoon? We were thru-hikers of the Appalachian Trail, only a few yards from the "footpath," eating hot McDonald's hamburgers with ice cold beverages. I felt content. This was one of those pivotal moments of my entire journey. I experienced a kind of internal satisfaction as I enjoyed my lunch. With more confidence than I had had at any time since leaving Springer, I realized that I could quite possibly make it all the way to Baxter State Park with minimal inconvenience, at least after dark that is. The thought brought another smile to my face as I discarded my trash in a waste basket before heading back to the trail.

As the afternoon progressed Banzai separated himself from Pilgrim and me. By the time we reached the Wiley home, he was lounging in the yard enjoying one of Marilyn's treats. The "Cookie Lady" regularly provides weary hikers with her tasty sweets. Roy brought out a fresh batch so that Pilgrim and I could also indulge before the ride to Pittsfield.

My two travelling companions and I concluded our day with a meal at a Friendly's, located only a few yards from the Quality Inn where we decided to share a room for the night. The younger Banzai was seldom opposed to sleeping on the floor for a reduced rate. Pilgrim and I didn't mind paying a little more for the two beds. What mattered more continued to be the opportunity to sleep indoors and carry light packs.

Day 112 began with another surprise. Rather than Roy, the "Cookie Lady" appeared to shuttle us back to the A.T. at Washington Mountain Rd. Like the previous day, the Wileys would give us the opportunity to slackpack again. The plan called for a rendezvous in Cheshire, Massachusetts, one of the towns that the trail passes through. From there we would drive to Williamstown, MA, where we would set up another "base" from which to slackpack for two days. The following day we could hike to MA 2 from Cheshire and return to our motel for a second night. All we would have to do was arrange for the shuttles.

On today's hike my buddies and I again had the good fortune to enjoy a hot lunch. Rather than at a picnic table just off the trail, this time it was at the Dalton Café in Dalton, MA. From Washington Mountain Rd. Banzai, Pilgrim, and I covered the 9.5 miles to Dalton in just over four hours. We first stopped at the home of A.T. legend Tom Levardi, a trail angel of the truest sense who has been allowing hikers to camp in his yard for over thirty years. After hearing about our hikes, Tom accepted our invitation to join us for lunch.

Tom also suggested that we hike on from his home to where the trail heads up High St. He would pick us up there, take us to the café and then return us to the spot we left the trail. This certainly seemed like a great plan to all of us. Our newfound friend even offered to take Pilgrim to the post office to pick up a package.

Over lunch I went into more detail about my method of hiking. Somewhat amused by all the nights I was spending in motels, and all the hot food I was eating, Tom agreed to help with the plan by providing a shuttle the following morning. We knew that Roy or Marilyn Wiley would be picking us up at the end of the day, but until now we didn't know how we would get back to Cheshire to continue the hike. Tom solved that problem.

For the remainder of the 18.3 miles, I hiked in good spirits. We culminated the slackpack day with a stop at an ice cream shop on the outskirts of town. Pilgrim ordered a root beer float. The lady handed him only a cup filled with vanilla ice cream.

A bit befuddled, Pilgrim asked, "Where's the root beer?"

"Behind you," she replied expressionless. "In the refrigerator."

Apparently, you had to make your own float. I ordered the same. After pouring the cold beverage over my ice cream, there was still enough in the bottle for a long drink. The creamy treat hit the spot after a weary day on the trail. Yes, I was tired. Even though the three of us were eating well and sleeping in beds, we were still hiking a lot of miles every day. The mountains still had to be climbed; the streams still had to be crossed; and the weather conditions still had to be dealt with. My method definitely afforded us some conveniences, and what others may even consider luxuries, but still the trail was the trail, and hiking the Appalachian Trail is tough.

So after another long day of hiking, Pilgrim, Banzai, and I shuttled up to Williamstown, MA with Marilyn Wiley. Williamstown is a bit on the expensive side, as A.T. towns go; however, we found a modest motel on the outskirts of town for a reasonable price. It also sat next to a small breakfast restaurant, the Chef's Hat. And within sight, less than a quarter mile up the highway, we spotted a steakhouse. The two establishments would provide our morning and evening meals over the next two days.

My two hiking buddies and I began my day 113 with pancakes, eggs, bacon, and coffee before driving back to the A.T. in Cheshire with Tom Levardi. We were all extremely grateful for the rather long shuttle that Tom provided. He dropped us in front of the post office where we had concluded the previous day's hike. From there we walked through the quaint village-like town together.

Eventually we came to where the trail headed back into the woods and were greeted with a steady climb of over 2000 feet. Since the ascent was gradual over five miles, and since the three of us had devoured a gigantic breakfast, we hiked energetically throughout the morning.

Around noon we ascended Mt. Greylock, the highest peak in Massachusetts. Atop Greylock sits Bascom Lodge. Private rooms, a bunkroom, and a restaurant are all housed within the rustic building. Carrying only slackpacks on a day we planned to spend the night back in Williamstown, we didn't need the sleeping accommodations. The restaurant, however, allowed us to enjoy a hot lunch for the third consecutive day.

"Who says thru-hiking the Appalachian Trail has to be drudgery?" Banzai noted as he bit into a large barbecue sandwich.

Pilgrim, Banzai, and I were definitely spending more money than the average A.T. hiker. But then again, it had been a long time since I had eaten trail food or stayed overnight in the woods. In fact, I was about to leave Massachusetts, having concluded every day of the state's 90 miles in a bed. I reminded myself that I had done the same in Connecticut. And if the next two weeks went as scheduled, my buddies and I would be duplicating the plan in Vermont.

During lunch I also arranged for a ride back to our motel. This time I consulted the shuttle list on the Appalachian Trail Conservancy website. From the choices I selected Ellen.

"Hello, I'm an A.T. thru-hiker. There are three of us who need a lift from MA 2 to the Villager Motel on the outskirts of town. Are you available in about three hours?'

"I think I can do that. Who are you?"

"I'm Mike. My trail name is Don's Brother."

"Don's Brother!" Ellen almost shouted in excitement. "I've been following your journal. Are Pilgrim and Banzai the other two hikers?"

"Yep. So you can help us out?"

"I'll be there waiting," Ellen cheerfully replied.

When we reached MA 2 at the Hoosic River, our trail angel was already there. We quickly found out that Ellen was previous thru-hiker Bagel. Not only had she arrived early, but she had brought with her enormous cookies and large bottles of juice for each of us. After a brief time of pleasant conversation, we drove back to our motel. When we tried to pay the sweet lady for her help, she adamantly refused. With all the money we were spending, Banzai, Pilgrim, and I greatly appreciated Bagel's generosity.

After a somewhat challenging 14.7 miles which included the ascent of Mt. Greylock, my buddies and I again had hot showers to look forward to. Then we concluded our day with another fine dining experience at the Cozy Corner, a family restaurant with lots of menu options. This seemed like the most appropriate of place names for a DBM meal at the end of a hiking day.

After a second night in the Williamstown motel, our plan for day 114 would take us to where the trail crosses VT 9, a little over five miles east of Bennington, Vermont. Our good fortune continued when I received a phone message from Steve, a resident of Bennington who had been reading my online journal.

"You're in my neck of the woods now," Steve's message conveyed. "Let me know how I can help you."

Since Steve and I had corresponded previously, I decided to give him a call. When I asked him if he thought he could come down to Williamstown and pick up our gear so that we could slackpack the following day, he eagerly agreed. Apparently Steve gets a great deal of personal satisfaction out of helping hikers. We were three of those hikers who were certainly grateful.

Before another trail angel's arrival, Banzai, Pilgrim, and I again consumed large quantities from the breakfast menu of the Chef's Hat. Banzai was getting a little concerned about spending so much money, even though he liked my method. Still, he was looking for some ways to cut costs. I could understand my young friend's concern. As I have previously stated, Pilgrim and I had retirement checks coming in each month. Banzai didn't.

With light packs and sandwiches in them for lunch, we embarked on the 18.4 mile day with a continued sense of resolve. Three states remained and the Don's Brother Method was in full throttle as we prepared to enter Vermont.

Even with large patches of thick, black mud to deal with, nothing on the trail could detract from the feeling of knowing that three nights awaited in Bennington's Catamount Motel. Steve recommended the hiker-friendly inn, and was waiting at VT 9 when we reached the intersection to take us there. The last mile's sharp elevation loss caused Pilgrim and me to slow dramatically. When we did arrive at the road, however, Steve was already there with a cooler of beverages. The ice cold Mountain Dew never tasted better on the hot, late afternoon.

Since my hiking partners and I had shared a room for the past three nights, we each decided to get our own for the first night in Bennington. With a very reasonable $50 rate, the clean, comfortable room at the Catamount seemed like a bargain.

Needing a little solitude, I declined Banzai and Pilgrim's invitation to join them for dinner. Instead, I did some writing first before walking up the street to a neighborhood Friendly's. It kind of felt nice again to dine alone in a town that I'd visited on four other occasions. Knowing that the following day would be a day off after 18 consecutive days on the trail also brought a smile to my face. All was going reasonably well as I headed to Maine using the Don's Brother Method.

CHAPTER 13

Vermont Lodging

We get lots of requests for slacking and staying an extra night in town. Part of the issue for NOBO's is that by the time a hiker reaches Vermont, the body hurts all over.

Jeff Taussig, The Green Mountain House Hostel (Manchester Center, VT)

Before hiking our first full day in Vermont, Banzai and Pilgrim both agreed with me that a zero day was needed. My last day of rest had been when I took the train into New York City to visit my daughter. That trip originated in Port Jervis, the town closest to where the trail passes High Point State Park in New Jersey. In other words, I had hiked through part of New Jersey and all of New York, Connecticut, and Massachusetts since my last day off. That's 274 trail miles and a lot of scaled mountains since I had enjoyed a full day's rest.

I used day 115 to do a little sightseeing in Bennington, do my laundry, eat, and just relax. The morning began with what seems to be becoming my "regular" breakfast….bacon, eggs, toast, and coffee. I haven't been able to locate any grits lately; however, I've occasionally rounded out my meal with a side of hash browns. The Blue Benn Diner served up some of the best victuals I've had since leaving Georgia.

Mid-way through the afternoon, Pilgrim, Banzai, and I also discussed how to continue with the DBM over the next 40.1 miles of trail. This would prove to be one of our greatest logistical challenges since there are only two navigable roads in this entire stretch.

When we approached Steve about picking us up at USFS Rd. 71, he again happily agreed. The only caveat, however, was that he couldn't get there until after he got off work, which would be around 8:00 PM. We said that we didn't mind. With this plan we could slackpack the 20.6 miles and again return to Bennington for one final night in a Catamount bed.

My buddies and I concluded our off day by joining Steady and Spirit for a meal at the Madison Brew Company on Main St. I had honestly lost count of the number of days that I had consumed large portions of town food to begin and to end my day. Even with the massive number of calories I was ingesting, I had still lost over twenty pounds. This is evidence of how important nutrition is when thru-hiking the Appalachian Trail. The more food one takes in, the stronger he hikes.

Steve arrived early on the morning of day 116 to return Banzai, Pilgrim, and me to the A.T. at VT 9. Before departing from Bennington, however, we made a brief stop at the golden arches. Not only did we begin our day with a big breakfast, but we also carried an assortment of McDonald's fast food in our packs for lunch. My buddies had also adopted my practice of bringing along a soft drink as well.

Even though we were again slackpacking, the 20.6 miles of varied terrain was hard. We took breaks at three of the four shelters along this section, yet the climbs were challenging on another hot, buggy day. After passing so many roads and trail towns in Connecticut and Massachusetts, the trail seemed downright lonely on this first full day in Vermont. One portion of *The A.T. Guide* lists absolutely nothing for six miles. I couldn't recall any other time when so much isolation existed. We encountered only three other hikers all day.

We finally reached USFS Rd. 71 shortly before dark. It was a bit unnerving to think that we had no gear with which to stay in the woods if there were an issue with our shuttle. We had, in fact, put all our faith in Steve. So

The Don's Brother Method

it was no wonder that my buddies and I felt a sense of relief when we heard the motor of an oncoming vehicle. I don't know what I was happiest to see….. Steve and his car, or the cooler of cold drinks he had in its trunk.

One of the obvious drawbacks to the Don's Brother Method of hiking the Appalachian Trail revolves around long shuttles. The drive back to Bennington would take over an hour. And of course, we would have to return to this spot to continue the hike the next day. Still, town food, a hot shower, and a comfortable bed were the tradeoff.

Before leaving us at the Catamount, Steve suggested that he shuttle our gear up to Manchester Center so that we could slackpack again tomorrow. We had called ahead to make reservations with Jeff for two nights at his very popular Green Mountain House hostel. I got the impression that Steve had offered this service before. His generosity and kindness far surpassed any of our initial expectations. Even though our Bennington trail angel tried to refuse our money, Pilgrim, Banzai, and I insisted that he take what we offered. At least it would cover the cost of a tank of gas.

On the morning of day 117 my hiking partners and I had to say a final goodbye to our home for three days and to a wonderful friend. After another quick stop at McDonald's, we were on our way back to the trail. Arriving back at USFS Rd. 71, I wondered what percentage of A.T. thru-hikers had used this road to shuttle. I doubted if it were even five percent. Still, with a pre-arranged pick-up, it can be done. This is definitely not a road from which to hitch. But as I've already stated, it's one of only two exits over the 40.1 miles between VT 9 near Bennington and VT 11 and 30 leading into Manchester Center. The other road option is Stratton-Arlington Rd., two miles farther up the trail.

After another reasonably challenging, 19.5 mile day, which included the climb over Stratton Mountain, the three of us reached the road crossing by late afternoon. We scored a lift into town with a day-hiker from the area.

We ate at another Italian place and then called Jeff for a ride to the hostel. All the beds were filled inside the main structure, so Pilgrim, Banzai, and I were relegated to the bunkhouse out back. Even though there was no indoor plumbing, the bunks were comfortable and sheets were provided. The sleeping accommodations still far surpassed A.T. shelters, and we had use of all the home amenities until bedtime.

I would highly recommend Jeff's Green Mountain House. I would also suggest that you call ahead for reservations. During the busiest time of thru-hiker season, it stays full. Plus, there will already be some southbounders in the region by mid-July. If no space is available, there are other places to find a bed in Manchester Center. Some services in this upscale New England town, however, can prove fairly expensive.

Like with the two previous towns, we decided to keep our sleeping accommodations for a second night in Manchester Center. And like Steve, Jeff was happy to stop for fast food on our way back to the trail at VT 11 the following morning. Over the past week Pilgrim, Banzai, and I had ordered just about every item on the McDonald's breakfast menu. On more than one occasion I began my hike holding both trekking poles in one hand and a cup of coffee in the other. Day 118 was one of them.

With a positive attitude in tow and the thought of an indoor bunk and town food at the end of another hiking day, even the climbs seemed less taxing. First came Bromley Mountain and white blazes on a ski slope. That section was followed by Mad Tom Notch, which prompted Banzai and me to compose a folk song tribute to Mad Tom on the spot. We weren't sure who Mad Tom was. I suppose we were just looking for distractions to fill some time. Regardless, our loosely constructed lyrics may be found in my other book, *Don's Brother*.

Later in the afternoon, Pilgrim, Banzai, and I encountered arguably one of the toughest sections in Vermont: Baker Peak. Spoon, a hiker whom Banzai had met weeks earlier, appeared to join us for the ascent of the slanted, often jagged, rocks. Part of me felt grateful for the challenge, especially with the White Mountains of New Hampshire just over the horizon. Another part would have rather been walking on a pine-straw laden path.

Over the next almost five miles we passed three shelters, including Big Branch, where we took a short break. After the brief rest we quickly made our way to Danby-Landgrove Rd. Jeff waited with cold drinks for each of us. On the drive back to the town, Jeff also stopped at a local market where my buddies and I bought ingredients for a home-cooked meal. With all the restaurant

The Don's Brother Method

food we have been ingesting, no one objected when I offered to prepare a spaghetti dinner at the hostel.

Day 118 ended around the dinner table at the Green Mountain House. For the past four months I had consumed a vast variety of foods in a number of fast food places as well as sit-down-and-order restaurants. And on a few occasions I had reluctantly eaten trail food. Tonight, however, was the first that I had prepared a full meal myself. I said a blessing of thanks for this opportunity that I had to hike the A.T. I also offered up gratefulness for my ability to continue walking north on most days with a light pack and a bed awaiting at the end of the hiking day. With the Don's Brother Method working so smoothly, all was well on the Appalachian Trail.

Day 119 again commenced with a stop by McDonald's before the shuttle back to the trail. It would be our last in Manchester Center. Banzai, Pilgrim, and I said goodbye to Jeff and thanked him for his hospitality at the trailhead. After 2.2 miles of a scheduled 14.8 mile day, we stopped briefly at the Little Rock Pond Shelter. Spoon, who had tented there the previous night, re-joined our trio for the remainder of the day.

Even though I carried my full pack for the trek to VT 103, I took comfort in my expectations of Rutland. On my section-hike of Vermont, Alton and I had stayed two nights in the city of approximately 60,000.

I remembered a somewhat annoyed taxi driver's reply back in 2007 when I asked, "How large a town is Rutland?"

"Rutland isn't a town; it's a city!"

Aware that Rutland offered a plethora of motels from which to choose and many dining establishments within walking distance of most, I knew with certainty that this moderately-sized "city" would be a suitable base for the next two nights.

Even though a shorter mileage day was on our agenda, the heat and humidity made it tough. At least I had a fast food lunch in my heavier-than-usual pack. At VT 140, my three buddies and I paused to enjoy our meal. Spoon's quick wit complimented the more serious sides of Banzai and Pilgrim. His stories also provided diversion over the ascent of yet another Bear Mountain, the third since Connecticut.

The almost 1100 foot elevation gain would not have been that difficult on a cooler day. Today, however, we were challenged. Perhaps it was the fat content of our lunch, or maybe it was simply the heat, but I struggled throughout much of the afternoon.

At the Minerva Hinchey Shelter we rested briefly. This was the first day in a while when we didn't have a pre-arranged ride at the end of the hike. That changed when I noticed a poster, with a name and phone number, taped to a wall of the structure. A little later I phoned Tom to arrange for a shuttle into Rutland from the trailhead at VT 103. He arrived only a few minutes after we did. Spoon had no interest in going into town, so Banzai, Pilgrim, and I wished him well on his night in the woods before tossing our gear into the trunk of Tom's car.

After stopping at two motels that couldn't meet our requests, we opted for a Quality Inn on Main Street, only a block from a 99 restaurant. There is a hostel in Rutland, but on the Don's Brother Method, motels are always preferable.

We decided on two rooms rather than one since we would be adding a fourth member to our group on the morn. Banzai had convinced his college professor brother, Mike, that providing us support with a car was a perfect way to spend the two weeks leading up to his fall semester. Banzai also enticed his twin with the promise of free rooms, meals, and gas for his vehicle while he fulfilled the role of our "private" shuttle driver.

It looked like a winning situation for all of us. Mike would get to visit with old friends in New Hampshire, hike some himself, and live "freely" (in more ways than one) for about a fortnight. Banzai, Pilgrim, and I would have the luxury of knowing that we would have a ride waiting at the trailhead at the end of each day for the remainder of the trail in Vermont and the southern section of New Hampshire, including the first few days in the Whites.

None of us could seem to stop smiling over our steaks and baked potatoes at 99 later in the evening. Were it not for Banzai's caveman-like beard, Pilgrim's almost emaciated physique, and my shaggy hair, our waitress might not have even known that we were A.T. hikers. We always seemed to get a few stares in restaurants, even in trail towns, or in the case of Rutland, trail cities.

The Don's Brother Method

Day 120 began a new episode in the Don's Brother Method of thru-hiking the Appalachian Trail. With a full-time driver, we no longer had to seek out rides to towns after days in the woods, or back to the trail after nights in beds. On this first day with Mike (the college professor who nixed our idea of the obvious trail name), we stopped at a diner for breakfast in route back to the trailhead at VT 103.

On an 18.4 mile, cooler, damp day, I hiked with enjoyment, especially knowing that there would be no nights planned for the woods over the next several days. That enjoyment was especially enhanced early in the afternoon, when I saw Fatty for the first time since Pennsylvania. After spending over a week without a night off the trail, the vivacious Canadian blond accepted our offer of a place to sleep in Rutland.

With a day that included a climb of over 3000 feet up Mt. Killington, Pilgrim, Banzai, Fatty, and I reached US 4 well before sundown. Mike chatted with a trail angel who had quite a spread laid out, including a cooler filled with Klondike bars. Even though they were partially melting, our little group quickly devoured a dozen or so of the ice cream treats.

Even though it was a bit of a tight squeeze getting all of us, including the slender Fatty, into Mike's compact, with the thought of a hot meal and soft pillow in our futures, no one complained. In fact, smiles abounded over another feast later in the evening. Old hiking friend Steady, and his wife Spirit, joined our little group for supper at 99. I just wanted to enjoy the fellowship rather than dwell on another long day that awaited.

Beds and bunks continued to prevail on days 101-120 of my quest to reach Katahdin. For the 20 day period I spent only one night in the woods. That is, if the cinder block RPH shelter, at the edge of a neighborhood and adjacent to a road, where pizza is delivered, can be considered "the woods."

Day 121 started with a breakfast in Rutland before the ride back to the trailhead. With an unexpected challenging climb up Quimby Mountain early in the day, and 22.3 miles on the agenda, my buddies and I were grateful to be well-nourished. Mike joined us for the early part of today's hike, and then after a few miles, re-traced his path back to his car. He plans to do out-and-back hikes, as well as some sight-seeing, before picking us up at our stopping point each day.

Like most other days, Banzai, Pilgrim, and I carried town food lunches in our packs. We dined sitting on rocks just off the trail. Trudging on throughout the afternoon, we eventually connected with Mike at VT 12 which leads to Woodstock. The small Vermont town offers a couple of pricey motels; however, we decided to spend one more night in Rutland. There are definitely major advantages to having a car at one's disposal. Even though the trip from and back to the A.T. would be longer, we saved money on the accommodations and were able to spend another night in the same rooms.

After two meals of somewhat upscale dining at the 99, the four of us chose less expensive fast food on our final night in Rutland. We also discussed our options for the next few days. Since Susquehanna Slim was expected to join our happy band of hikers for our last day in Vermont, I suggested moving our base up to White River Junction, a town offering more motel choices, and located just across the river from Hanover, New Hampshire. All agreed.

On the morning of day 122, Mike first stopped at a country store, where we enjoyed breakfast sandwiches and purchased take-out lunches before heading back to VT 12. Banzai's brother, a name we had attached to our shuttle provider, had his own itinerary. He planned to drive to Pomfret Rd., a little over four miles up the trail, hike south to meet us, and then hike back to his car with the group. Mike wanted to experience the trail without fully "experiencing" the trail. Still, we were grateful for his presence.

We would next see Mike at VT 14 a little later in the afternoon. I had instructed him to pick us up at a parking area near the I-89 underpass, 0.7 miles farther up the trail. Where he waited, however, was just across from the White River. Since a light drizzle had begun, no one squabbled over prematurely ending the day's hike. We would just have to cover 9.9 miles the following day rather than the 9.2 scheduled.

Despite cramped conditions inside the Mazda, none of us complained about the hiker scents of others. At least we were getting daily showers. We alternated who would sit where during transport, and even after some challenging days on the trail, Banzai, Pilgrim, and I always seemed pretty agreeable with each other.

From VT 14 the four of us headed into White River Junction and another Super 8 motel. Shortly after checking in, I re-acquainted myself with Susquehanna Slim, a fellow A.T. thru-hiker that I had first met in Erwin, TN and then again in Salisbury, CT. Sensing that Slim was struggling a bit when I last saw him, I had sent him an email with an invitation to join our small caravan for the final two states.

Near exhaustion, he had gone home to rest a few days. Then after recovering, the New Jersian replied to my message:

"Now that I have enough energy to be excited about anything, I'm very excited about playing D'Atagnan to the Three Musketeers and would love to join your merry band. I am committed to the Mid-Atlantic area until 7/20, so over the next week I'll be mosquito bait somewhere between the Delaware Water Gap and Kent, CT. On 7/22 I can get myself dropped off at a point to meet with you guys. We can go through the Whites and ME, and summit Katahdin together. Then I'll deal with the missing miles while you guys do the morning TV circuit."

I knew from Slim's note that he would be a perfect fit for our entourage.

He concluded in his email, "Thank you for extending this offer to me. I think it's going to really help me get the most out of this part of the trail."

That evening Slim accompanied Pilgrim and me for a meal at a Chinese restaurant a few hundred yards from the motel. The buffet offered us a wide variety of succulent selections. We all got to know each other a little better and roughly put together a tentative plan to take us through the Whites. Even though Banzai and his brother had chosen to dine with some friends of theirs who lived nearby, I felt certain they would approve of our strategies.

The next morning we started our day at a Dunkin Donuts just across the highway from the Super 8. I knew the breakfast sandwich, coffee, and two donuts would suffice for all the nutrients I would need for the short day. Banzai didn't seem too happy to be preparing to hike in what looked like a steady rain all morning. I reminded him that it would be our last day in Vermont.

So on day 123 I now had the company of three other thru-hikers, and I couldn't have been happier. Slim and Banzai seemed to hit it off rather quickly. From a short distance behind, I could hear the young scholar beginning one of his lectures for a new audience of one.

The morning passed rapidly. By midday we had slugged our way through the rain and reached the neighborhood streets of Norwich, VT. A mile and a half later we marched across the Ledyard Bridge that spans the Connecticut River. From there we made our way past the white blazes on telephone poles to Main Street in Hanover, New Hampshire.

Mike arrived shortly after we had hiked into town to drive us back to White River Junction. After hot showers, we all returned to Hanover for lunch at Molly's. Later in the evening our group was treated to a spaghetti supper at the home of Short 'n Sweet and Graybeard. The couple, who live right on the trail in Norwich, have been providing trail magic since their son thru-hiked back in 2007. Here I would also retrieve my sleeping bag which I had mailed ahead from Salisbury. Despite being offered overnight accommodations in their garage, we graciously declined, having already booked another night at the Super 8.

CHAPTER 14

The Huts of New Hampshire and Some Motels As Well

The DBM removes a lot of misery from hiking. Recovering every night at hotels means that you can push harder during the day. You smell better, you feel better, you eat better, you carry less weight, and you just have a better time. It's not for everyone, but neither is pitching a tent.

MICHAEL DOUMA, BANZAI'S BROTHER (ARLINGTON, VA)

MY DAY 124 BEGAN WITH one of the top five breakfasts of the entire hike. Lou's restaurant and bakery has occupied its place on Main Street in Hanover, and directly on the A.T., since 1947. Not only did my hiking companions and I eat heartily from an assortment of eggs, bacon, sausage, toast, and potatoes, but we also each received a complimentary pastry for being thru-hikers.

The visit to Lou's proved to be a fitting way for the gang to begin its first full day in New Hampshire. I use the word "gang" here in reference to how my buddies and I began referring to ourselves. After singing a few verses of the old theme song from a 1960's western, "Rawhide," we had good-naturedly begun to call our band the "Rawhide gang." With Banzai's brother as our shuttle driver, we were enthusiastically "rolling, rolling, rolling" up the Appalachian Trail.

After leaving the downtown area of Hanover, Banzai, Pilgrim, Susquehanna Slim, and I first had to walk past white-blazed telephone poles along tree-lined streets on the campus of Dartmouth College, before heading back into the woods. The trail for the first New Hampshire day resembled the trail of Vermont, especially with its abundance of thick black mud. I took two falls today, my first in a couple of weeks. The second was due to the icky substance. Regardless of the oozing sections of muddy trail, no other significant obstacles appeared.

At the conclusion of a 17.5 mile day we chose to drive back to White River Junction for one final night. Since there were no suitable motels in the area of Dorchester Rd., where we concluded the day's hike, it seemed the logical choice. Long drives after a day's hike sometimes become a necessity when using the Don's Brother's Method. Yes, my buddies and I were getting a bit spoiled with the hot showers, soft pillows, and bountiful buffets.

After another restful night's sleep, we began day 125 back at Dorchester Rd. I can't overemphasize how significant having a full time driver was during this stage of our journey. It was quite a distance back to the A.T. from White River Junction. If we had needed to find a local who provided shuttles, it could have proven very expensive. In fact, if Mike had not been with us, we may have had to stay in Hanover in order to continue using my method. White River Junction isn't really a "trail town" as such. As with other long shuttles, however, it can be done. It just requires planning.

Today we got our first taste of what we think the Whites will offer. Cube Mountain provided some of the best views since the Smokies. Even though a few craggy rocks slowed our pace, the 16.0 mile day seemed to go by quickly.

When Banzai, Pilgrim, Slim, and I reached NH 25A, a paved road 4.8 miles west of Wentworth, NH, Mike was waiting. Our plan again called for a lengthy drive into Lincoln where we would again set up a "base camp" for the next few days. This practice worked well throughout the hike. I had first utilized the method on day four back at Hogpen Gap. Now in my 13th A.T. state, I still preferred it.

Before choosing a motel for the next three nights, the gang stopped along route 112 for pizza. We shared three large pies and discussed options for the next few days. Tomorrow would be our final day before heading into the spectacularly beautiful, yet treacherous, White Mountains. We all exhibited a touch of what might be referred to as "excited anticipation." Deep down, I felt fear.

The Don's Brother Method

Rather than staying at one of the motels in the center of town, my buddies and I instead chose to drive up US 3 where other establishments were located. After checking rates at a couple of locally owned places, we selected a Roadway Inn. The rooms were adequate and the price seemed reasonable for the touristy area. I rested well in my bed, although I occasionally thought of the many thru-hikers I had met over the past four months who seldom frequented a motel. I knew that many, maybe most, preferred the woods. In no way did I miss my tent as I adjusted my blanket before quickly falling asleep.

The gang began day 126 with another enormous breakfast at the Longhorn Palace Pancake House. Located across the road from our motel, its menu offered just about everything one could imagine. With only a short 9.9 mile day scheduled, none of us saw any need to hurry. Our pleasant waitress refilled our coffee cups often while we listened to one of Professor Mike's lectures. I suspect that at times each of us experienced varying degrees of irritability or impatience with one another. Yet, we knew that we needed each other for the Don's Brother Method to work efficiently. Earlier in my hike I had travelled solo over 400 miles without spending a night in the woods. Now I was grateful to have companions.

When we did finally finish the meal, the five of us again packed into the Mazda for the drive back to NH 25A. Situating our packs on our laps, Slim, Pilgrim, and I tightly compressed ourselves into the back. We alternated who would get the comfort of the front passenger seat. Today it was Banzai's turn. Still, no one complained. After all, we had spent another night in a room and just filled ourselves with bacon and eggs. It was all good.

On this shorter distance day, we often ambled. With the exception of a break at Mt. Mist, we hiked over the rocks, roots, and mud without lingering. Like other days, Banzai's brother hiked south to meet us about a mile before we arrived at the road. Just past noon the group reached NH 25 where we would end the day's hike.

The Hikers Welcome Hostel, located just a few yards up the highway, offers shuttles and slackpacking options. Had the gang not had Mike to provide our transportation, I'm quite sure that we would have used its services for a day or two. The proprietor also provides rides into Warren, NH, five miles east, for long-term re-supply. We stopped to get some information before heading back to town. Lunch at a restaurant, a hot shower, and a stroll around Lincoln awaited.

Later in the evening I talked by phone with my good friend Alton. For the past few days he had been sending me texts and emails suggesting that our group hike south over Mt. Moosilauke. The tenor of some of his messages bordered on pleas. He had hiked this section the previous spring and knew of the steep descent off the crest of the mountain. Hiking up a dangerous part of trail almost always poses less difficulty than hiking down. Still, I wasn't sold on his suggestion.

Since I had left Springer Mountain I had only hiked north. Many thru-hikers choose to do a southbound segment occasionally for a variety of reasons. Sometimes it regards a shuttle; at others, it involves the severity of a climb or descent. Whatever the reason, hiking south for a day is often an option. For me it wasn't.

Each of my buddies had done some southbound segments already and were happy to approach Moosilauke in either direction.

"Maybe your friend Alton has a point," Susquehanna Slim noted as he perhaps picked up on the trepidation in my eyes.

"No, I've hiked every step north thus far, and I plan to continue."

Knowing how important it was for me to keep my promise to myself, all three of my hiking companions agreed. No one really seemed to care in which direction we were going to hike the following morning. All that we really were concerned about was our readiness for the White Mountains of New Hampshire.

So on day 127, after another large robust breakfast, the gang set out for where we had ended the previous day's hike at NH 25 near Glencliff. Despite an elevation gain of almost 4000 feet over five and one-half miles, we all managed to hike happily on a mild, sunny, gorgeous morning. My McDonald's hamburgers, which I had purchased in Lincoln, never tasted so good when I consumed them on the peak of Moosilauke.

This was unquestionably my kind of hiking. A large country breakfast, burgers for lunch on the top of a 4,802 foot mountain with panoramic views, and another restaurant meal waiting for me later in the afternoon. Then I could top it all off with an additional night in a motel. Today's 9.3 miles didn't actually constitute "big miles," but the light pack and bed certainly were a part of the formula.

After the leisurely lunch atop Mt. Moosilauke, our much-anticipated descent awaited. With deliberation and numerous pauses to rest and regain my composure, I successfully made my way down the dangerously steep, sometimes slick mountain and continued northward on the A.T. toward Kinsman Notch. I stopped to read the warning sign at the trailhead before walking on to a parking lot where Mike's car was waiting.

THIS TRAIL IS EXTREMELY TOUGH. IF YOU LACK EXPERIENCE, PLEASE USE ANOTHER TRAIL. TAKE SPECIAL CARE AT THE CASCADES TO AVOID TRAGIC RESULTS. I was sure glad to be standing in front of the sign *after* completing the section. And I was especially thankful that there had been no "tragic results."

When we arrived back in Lincoln, Mike, Banzai, Pilgrim, and Slim wanted to eat at a pizza place. Preferring to be alone for a while to reflect on my day and write, I instead walked up the street a block to a Subway. I sat alone for a couple of hours, enjoying my meal and then working on my journal entry for the day.

Eventually I strode back to meet my buddies. Having heard about a hostel in Lincoln from other thru-hikers, Banzai and Mike had decided that they would like to save a little money. Pilgrim, Slim, and I reluctantly agreed to join the brothers at Chet's Place. The hostel actually consisted of bunks in a garage, but since it was on a "donations accepted" policy, we slightly cut our costs for one night. We weren't in the woods, but in many ways I felt like I was in a shelter on the trail. The accommodations were rustic to say the least. Chet, however, was a genuinely nice individual.

Later in the evening I ate again. It had been a good day. I had consumed four meals of town food, completed the first day in the Whites, and had a bunk (even though it wasn't among my most comfortable), in which to rest. Turning in early, I began to think about the longer day we had planned for tomorrow. Just before falling to sleep I remember wondering if I were ready.

Twenty-four hours later all I could say was that I survived. Day 128 goes down as the most difficult and tiring of any of the 164 days that I would eventually wind up hiking to complete my thru-hike of the Appalachian Trail. It was brutal. It was scary. It left me feeling more fatigued than I had felt any day since leaving Springer Mountain.

Knowing that the planned 16.3 mile hike would require every possible minute of daylight, my buddies and I were waiting in the parking lot of the Lincoln McDonald's when it opened at 5:00 AM. Fifty minutes later we were walking back up the trail. For the next fourteen hours I would climb and descend, often grabbing tree limbs for balance. I fell, I bled, and I struggled to maintain my sanity on this most challenging of days. I describe the day in great detail in *Don's Brother*. For now, I'll just say that I survived.

When I finally reached Franconia Notch, wet, cold, bloody, and exhausted, I felt beyond grateful to have this section of trail behind me. I felt equally grateful to have a ride back to a motel where a bed awaited. I'm certain my friends felt the same. Not much was said in the cramped Mazda on the drive back to Lincoln in a steady drizzle. We were just too tired to talk.

Fortunately, our plan called for a return to a motel for the next two nights. After a quick stop for hot showers and clean clothes, we travelled to a steakhouse for a very late supper. It was past 10:30 when I first cut into my juicy, thick sirloin. Recapping the day's events and realizing that our bodies had taken a beating, all of us agreed that a day of rest was in order. I hadn't had a zero day since Bennington, 205 miles earlier. I needed a break, and the following day would afford me one.

Waking in the comfort of a motel room, my first thought was, "I don't have to hike today." Still, I needed to write. Yesterday had been the first that I had not written about my day before turning in for the night. Even when staying in shelters, I had always written. On most occasions I had been fortunate to have a cell phone signal to publish to my journal. The previous night I was just too exhausted. After the late steak dinner, it was past midnight when we reached our rooms.

All of the group wanted to take full advantage of this rest day. Plans were made to go back into Lincoln in the afternoon for some shopping. I needed to buy new hiking shorts and had also decided to get rubber tips for my trekking poles. But before the trip to town, I ventured out to a gazebo in front of the motel to write. Looking up at the mountains in the distance, I was grateful to be a couple of thousand feet lower on the morning of day 129.

Changes were on the horizon, however, for day 130. For the first time since Banzai and Pilgrim had joined me in Great Barrington, MA, there appeared to be no way to avoid sleeping on the A.T. for a night. From Kinsman Notch to Grafton Notch in the White Mountain National Forest, the Appalachian Mountain Club (AMC) maintains a series of huts for overnight stays. They are usually stone buildings that sleep from around 50 to over 100 in bunk rooms. Although rather expensive if one wants a bed, thru-hikers can sometimes get a "work for stay" option. You don't get a bunk, but are permitted to sleep on the floor in the dining part of the facility after all the paying guests have vacated the area. Leftover food is also provided gratis.

Surprisingly, many of the huts are filled to capacity with folks who had hiked up one of the many trails (other than the A.T.) in the Whites. Most stay for only a night. A crew of college-aged young people fulfill various tasks at the huts throughout the summer months. They cook, clean, and even entertain after supper. Even though showers aren't available, running water and toilets are. They are definitely a step up from shelters.

Without a highway from which to "escape" the woods for the next 27.4 miles, Banzai, Pilgrim, Slim and I agreed to break the next section into two days with an overnight stay at Galehead Hut. The 13.0 mile stretch on the first day again was tedious, taking me over twelve hours to complete. Late in the afternoon Banzai hiked ahead to make sure he could secure one of the "work for stay" slots. Some huts only allow two or three; others will permit any thru-hiker to stay as long as room is available.

It was almost dark, however, before Pilgrim, Slim, and I made our way down a treacherous Mt. Garfield to Galehead. Even though we were happy that the younger Banzai was going to be able to sleep for free, none of us complained about the almost triple digit charge for space in a bunkroom. After all, it was a bed and the fee did include a hot evening meal as well as a large breakfast.

Day 131 was the first that I had begun without needing a ride back to the trail since the RPH shelter back in New York. That was 401.2 trail miles and 29 days earlier. Using my Don's Brother Method, I had hiked through Connecticut, Massachusetts, Vermont, and 82 miles of New Hampshire without spending a night directly on the A.T. Since the huts are really more like hostels, I've not included them as a "night in the woods."

With a 14.7 mile day scheduled, our plans were to meet Mike at Crawford Notch by late afternoon. Even though the trail still required some rock scrambling, the difficulty level overall for today's hike had been reduced. In fact, the final three miles before reaching US 302 were some of the most pleasant we had seen lately. At the end of the day it was good to reunite with Mike and the Mazda.

From the notch the five of us travelled into Gorham, NH for another night at a motel. As was the case in Lincoln, the prices in Gorham far surpassed lodging in the south; however, we were able to book two rooms at a moderately priced establishment. Sadly, tomorrow would be the last day that our group would benefit from our private shuttle provider. Mike had to return to his professorship, leaving Banzai, Pilgrim, Slim, and me the responsibility of finding our own transportation to and from the trail for the immediate future.

After dropping us back at Crawford Notch on the morning of day 132, Banzai's brother hit the road for Virginia. Needing to reach Lakes of the Clouds hut well before dark, we again scheduled an early start for the 11.2 mile day. The gang could not have had a more beautiful day to experience the Presidential Range of Mts. Jackson, Pierce, Eisenhower, and Monroe. For most of the day we hiked above 4000 feet with views in all directions.

Less than a mile prior to reaching the hut, however, the clouds rolled in. Visibility went from around one hundred miles to one hundred yards, and then one hundred feet, within minutes. We had been warned of the drastic weather shifts in the Whites, but still none of us expected to literally be walking in the clouds only a few minutes after sunshine had abounded.

Because of the dangerous conditions that sometimes prevail only 1.3 miles south of the Mt. Washington summit, it is rare that anyone will be turned away at Lakes of the Clouds. We were among around a dozen or so thru-hikers who were offered the "work for stay" option. Despite having to sleep in my sleeping bag on the floor, I was just grateful to be inside on a dreary, cold night. The meal was OK, and my job of re-binding old A.T. log books didn't seem too difficult. In fact, other than hot showers, the huts provide most of what hostels offer.

Before my buddies and I could depart Lakes of the Clouds the following morning, we were required to complete our "work for stay" agreement. I began day 133 sweeping out the bunkhouse rooms and putting away blankets. We were also given breakfast after all the paying guests had finished eating. Looking outside to see thick cloud-cover on the cold, damp August day, I don't think any of our group was that anxious to leave our warmer confines.

Eventually we departed the hut. Immediately faced with the ascent of 6,288 foot Mt. Washington, all of us realized that the 1.3 mile hike to the summit under the foggy conditions would require an hour or more. We were right. Almost exactly sixty minutes after walking out of the door of Lakes of the Clouds, we entered the snack bar atop the second highest peak on the Appalachian Trail. And of course a restaurant meant another meal.

While Banzai, Pilgrim, Slim, and I dined in the warmth of the Summit House, we discussed the weather conditions and our options for the remainder of the day. The original plan called for us to hike 5.7 miles farther up the trail to Madison Springs Hut.

"I think we should take the van down the mountain and wait until we get a better weather day before hiking off of Mt. Washington," I suggested to my companions.

Banzai didn't want to pay the $30 for shuttle service, and Slim hated to forfeit the remainder of the day. Pilgrim sided with me, and after only minimal discussion, the others bought in as well. On somewhat of a tighter budget than we three "old" guys, Banzai opted to hitch a ride down the Mount Washington Auto Road to Pinkham Notch. The rest of us paid, although Pilgrim and I did get a $5 senior discount. We were also informed that since we were thru-hikers, and leaving the mountain due to weather, that our tickets would be good for a return trip when we were ready to continue our hike.

When we reached the parking lot of the Pinkham Notch Visitor Center, we fortunately spied our old friends Spirit and Steady. Steady was about to hike north, but Spirit was going back into Gorham. She happily offered the four of us a ride to the same motel where we had stayed two nights earlier. Before our friend departed we arranged a time for her to take us back to Pinkham Notch the following morning.

Being back in town also afforded the gang the opportunity to discuss the next few day's itinerary over a restaurant meal. We were all a little concerned about the 30 degree wind chill and 50 MPH wind gusts forecast for the next day. Severe weather looked to be in the area for at least two more days. With that in mind, we all agreed that a change in plans was in order.

Since I had left Springer Mountain over four months ago, I had hiked every step north without any deviations in my plan. For the first time, however, it looked like that plan would need to be altered. Not wanting to return to Mt. Washington in the cold, wind and fog, we would have no alternative but to wait at least three days to continue our hike there. In order not to surrender any more days to weather, Slim had a suggestion.

"Let's start at Pinkham Notch tomorrow, hike the 21.1 miles over two days to US 2, and then return to Mt. Washington on Tuesday."

At first a little reluctant, I too soon realized that Slim's idea warranted merit. Even if we did alter the order of the miles we hiked, I would still be taking every step north.

"It makes sense," Pilgrim stated in support of Slim. "You can't see where to step on those damn rocks when you can't even see the damn rocks."

Laughing at our buddy's comment, Banzai, Slim, and I raised our glasses in a toast to the new plan.

After another comfortable night's sleep in a bed, I happily awoke early on day 134, wanting to enjoy every minute of another day off. Sprit arrived to take the group to McDonald's for breakfast. The Gorham Mickey D's was yet another that I had dined in on my thru-hike of the Appalachian Trail. At least a dozen came to mind.

While our group was enjoying our pancakes, Egg McMuffins, and an assortment of other fatty hiker favorites, in walked Johnny Walker, Gator,

Misery, and Puffy. The four young lads, that I had seen now and then going all the way back to North Carolina, joined our gang. Misery told of how they had spent the previous night in an abandoned house in the area. Ah, the bravado of youth! Johnny Walker also spoke of other adventures that the group had experienced recently on the trail. Even though the day's forecast called for more cold rain and high winds, they were heading back out.

When an invitation was issued to the only young member of our group to join them, Banzai couldn't resist. At first he seemed unsure. Then he declared that he wanted to hike ahead with his younger buddies. Susquehanna Slim, Pilgrim, and I said our goodbyes to our knowledgeable friend, wishing him well. I think we all hated to see him leave, yet at the same time we understood that he wanted to be around the young men closer to his age.

After breakfast, Spirit drove the now three of us to Walmart so that we could get some supplies. Since it would take two days to traverse the 21.1 miles from Pinkham Notch to US 2, we would need food for one night in the woods. It had been so long since I had actually "re-supplied," that I had some difficulty figuring out what to buy.

Spirit then dropped us at the Hiker's Paradise Hostel and Motel. We checked in with Bruno, the proprietor, and were escorted to the bunkrooms. Although not as tidy as a couple of other places I had stayed, this "paradise" met our minimum requirements, a bed and a bathroom. I selected an upper bunk in the front room which looked out onto the porch.

As lunchtime approached I decided to give Sweet Tooth a call. Thinking that Molar Man might be in the area, it occurred to me that the white Volvo also would. Diane was in Gorham. Seeming genuinely happy to hear from me, she agreed to meet us at a pizza place just up the road.

Over a late lunch, Sweet Tooth provided details of her and Molar Man's last few weeks. They had left the trail in New York and driven home to Ohio for the birth of another grandchild. Then Molar Man had resumed his hike in Vermont, with the plan to return there and hike south to where he had previously stopped in New York, after reaching Katahdin. For the past couple of weeks, the two had also continued to spend most nights in motels as he pursued the completion of his thru-hike. Sweet Tooth also told us that Molar

Man would be hiking off Mt. Washington on Tuesday as well. So if arrangements could be worked out, we would have another support driver for a while.

Things seemed to be continuing to go my way. Only two days after losing our full-time shuttler, it appeared that Pilgrim, Slim and I would be gaining another. As I've previously stated, the Don's Brother Method works a whole lot better when a guaranteed ride awaits at the end of each day's hike. Even though the roads would be scarce in Maine, I felt confident that if anyone could find them, Molar Man could. First, we needed to finish the Whites.

For the remainder of the day I just relaxed. In the late afternoon, I reclined in a worn, stuffed chair in the common area of the hostel. After the sun peeked through I wandered down the highway and found a bench on which to sit and write. Not knowing if or when I would see Banzai again, I felt a little sad. I would miss the young man's companionship. He had been a good hiking partner for almost four hundred miles.

That evening Slim, Pilgrim, and I walked to a Japanese Restaurant. I added yet another cuisine to my many dining experiences along the Appalachian Trail. The portions were plentiful and the tastes were quite good on another cold, August night in New Hampshire.

Day 135 began with a ride from Bruno back to Pinkham Notch. His small car in many ways resembled Mike's. We clutched our packs in our laps on the 10.7 mile commute. Bruno pointed out various peaks in the Wildcats, telling us that these slopes were his favorite places to ski. With some of our gear stashed back at the hostel, we planned to return to Hiker's Paradise two days later. Our driver said to call him and he would pick us up at US 2.

Before stepping back on the A.T., the three of us headed inside the visitor's center to partake of the breakfast buffet. Feeling a little queasy while thinking about potentially treacherous segments of trail, I for once didn't have much appetite. It took some coaxing from my mind to my stomach to get through a meal of sausage, eggs, cereal, and pastries. Most of those who were dining on the overcast, cold, windy morning were sightseers. In many ways I envied them.

Then I reminded myself that I only had one night in the woods before another night in Gorham. I smiled at the possibility of having the white Volvo for shuttles, perhaps until the end of my hike. Those thoughts would sustain me over the next 21.1 miles. I also recalled how quickly I had covered that same distance back in southern Virginia, finishing in less than nine hours. In this section of the Whites, however, we would still be travelling at no more than one mile per hour most of the time.

My foresight proved accurate as we soon found ourselves traveling up, over, and down Peaks E, D, C, and A of the Wildcat range. These climbs and descents were just as challenging as Kinsman and Garfield. They fatigued my brain. They left the backside of my new shorts wet and dirty from the many times I was forced to sit and slide down the dangerous slick rock faces.

Walking throughout the morning in a gusty wind, we reached Carter Notch Hut at 2:00. The warmth inside the oldest AMC-maintained structure on the A.T. brought comfort at a time when it was most needed. I quickly downed two cups of hot tea in an attempt to stop shivering. Slim and Pilgrim accepted bowls of black bean soup. None of us wanted to return immediately to the brutal conditions outside.

Knowing that trying to hike the remaining 6.9 miles to the Imp Shelter before dark looked impossible, we inquired about bunk space for the night. Even though $93 seemed steep, we happily paid the price. For us, spending the money far outweighed the "work for stay" option. I just wanted to enjoy hot food with the other paying guests and a warm bed to rest my weary body.

Wind howled throughout the night. In the pre-dawn Slim discovered a gust must have taken his pack cover which he had hung to dry on the porch of our bunkhouse.

Knowing that we still had a 14.9 mile day ahead, and unsure of just how severe the terrain would be, we began day 136 at 5:00. The crew prepared an early breakfast, fully aware of our potentially lengthy day.

Today was among the most challenging in New Hampshire. With wind gusts on the peaks of over 60 MPH and bone-chilling cold, at times I found it difficult to believe it was summer. Back in Georgia August daytime temperatures often hovered in the mid-90's. This felt more like January in the south.

Fortunately, the wind eventually subsided by late afternoon. We made our way from a maximum height of 4,832 feet at Carter Dome to 780 feet at US

2, reaching the road a little before 7:00. Bruno arrived within half an hour. Since he was driving a small truck with only room for one of us in the cab, Pilgrim and I chose to accept an offer of a ride from section-hiker, Rainman.

Back in Gorham, we vacated the hostel in lieu of a large Hiker's Paradise motel room with three beds. After hot showers we walked to a steakhouse for a late supper. I also called Molar Man to arrange a time for him and Sweet Tooth to meet us tomorrow. Pilgrim remembered a day back in Pennsylvania when Sweet Tooth had taken him to re-supply. Slim looked forward to meeting the dentist from Ohio. We welcomed the company of Molar Man and anticipated our good fortune in having his wife as our full-time support provider.

Day 137 began, like many on my Don's Brother's Method thru-hike, with breakfast at McDonald's. From there the five of us traveled back to the Mt. Washington Auto Road where we would take a van back up to the summit. Sweet Tooth had no intention of trying to navigate the winding road.

Back atop the mountain on a stellar weather day, we made our way to the sign that marks Mount Washington's peak. A park employee stated that this type of day only occurs around six times a year. Visibility on the cold, sunny blue-skied day was 120 miles. The views were simply beautiful.

At about 10:00 Molar Man, Slim, Pilgrim and I took our first steps down Washington. The boulders necessitated that I again hike deliberately. Within minutes my buddies were in the distance as each seemed to be having less difficulty with the terrain. As the cog railroad train passed, they waited for me to catch up.

"Don't wait for me," I let them know. I just wanted to make sure I didn't fall.

Molar Man and Slim quickly became friends and pace setters for our group. We even explained to Molar Man about our Rawhide theme. Although not seeming to overly embrace the idea, at least the serious, mild-mannered Ohioan accepted it.

Throughout the morning and early afternoon, the gang paused often to admire our stunning surroundings. We could not have been more fortunate than to experience such a magnificent day for hiking in the White Mountains.

Even the difficulty level did not diminish the beauty that surrounded us in all directions.

Still, it was late in the day before we reached Madison Spring Hut where we would spend the night. Because of the potential extreme weather conditions between Mts. Washington and Madison, it is unusual for anyone to be turned away at the hut. When given the option of "work for stay" or to pay $10 for the same lodging package minus the work, we all willingly chose to pay. About a half dozen other thru-hikers joined our group at a table somewhat isolated from the guests with reservations. The crew was even nice enough to heat our leftover food before serving us.

These huts are by no means as comfortable as a motel or even most hostels, but I was inside and had running water from a sink to brush my teeth. Really all that was missing was the shower. We were out of the elements on another extremely cold night. Despite reclining on two wooden benches I had pushed together, I slept well in my Western Mountaineering 10 degree bag on my Big Agnes mattress.

Anticipating another difficult day, I had little appetite the following morning. With full packs, Pilgrim and I walked into an early morning sunrise shortly before 7:00. Molar Man and Slim had already departed. From the outset Pilgrim hiked ahead. Kindly, he paused often to let me catch up.

Day 138 would be another when I hiked with deliberation. Throughout the ascent of Mt. Madison I meticulously selected rocks on which to step. Even a minor slip could have easily resulted in a sprained ankle or worse.

After reaching the peak of Madison, another painstakingly challenging descent awaited. Finally after hiking for over four hours, Pilgrim and I arrived below tree line. The trail continued to descend slightly until we reached Pinkham Notch. Bruno's wife, Maryann, shuttled us back to Hiker's Paradise where Slim had already secured another three-bedded room. Molar Man and Sweet Tooth had also taken a room at the motel. Later in the evening Slim, Pilgrim, and I dined at another steakhouse. With plans to spend the next two nights in the woods, we ate heartily.

A few hours later we added to those calories in McDonald's. With all the stops at the golden arches, I tended to alternate between the Big Breakfast,

Egg McMuffin Meal, and Hotcakes and Sausage. As I had other times over the past four months, I walked out of the fast food joint with a hot cup of coffee for the drive back to the A.T.

Despite having the sequence of my hike altered by delaying the Mt. Washington to Pinkham Notch section until after the Pinkham Notch to US 2 section, I was still only hiking north. After today there would be only one more state remaining. With that thought occupying my mind, I then also remembered that over 300 miles lay ahead.

As we headed toward US 2, 3.6 miles east of Gorham, I felt relieved that we were out of the White Mountain Range. Still, I realized that Maine would be equally tough. With all of our gear in tow, plans were to spend day 139 in the woods. Without tents, we knew that we needed to reach Gentian Pond shelter well before dark. Even though there appeared to be few thru-hikers in the vicinity, and the shelter slept fourteen, we didn't want to take any chances.

Seeming happy and content to have others with whom to share the trail, Molar Man had decided to forgo the North Carter section until after reaching Katahdin. Since he also had portions of the trail in MA, CT, and NY to complete as well, his plans were to hike that 21.1 mile stretch on his way back to Massachusetts. Knowing that I would have a support person in Sweet Tooth for the remainder of my thru-hike provided reassurance that there were still motels and restaurants to be enjoyed, even in remote Maine.

So as our four-member "Rawhide Gang" walked up a road portion of trail to begin our day, I felt content. My string of 38 days on the A.T. without spending the night in a shelter was about to be broken, but that was OK. After all, I realized that it would be highly unlikely that I could get all the way through Maine on the Don's Brother's Method. When I set foot on the trail today, over three weeks still remained.

We were greeted with a less-challenging trail, and it continued for most of the day. Being below tree line actually felt good. The spectacular views that we had enjoyed the past ten days were absent, but so was my trepidation. I hiked through most of the day without worry.

When we reached Gentian Pond shelter three others had already staked out the second level. Having no desire to join the group, I happily selected a downstairs spot next to the wall. One of the southbound hikers from above immediately engaged our group in conversation, offering much insight on what lay ahead. I blew up my mattress, got into my sleeping bag, and began to write. Within a short while the rain began.

The upstairs dweller continued to talk endlessly even though we all tried to ignore her. Having begun her hike on Katahdin a month earlier, she seemingly considered herself an authority on the A.T. in Maine. The lady also seemed to think it was her responsibility to share this knowledge with us.

"You will have to hike Goose Eye Mountain tomorrow," she informed us, as if we didn't have guide books. "It's really scary. I fell and almost killed myself," she noted, showing us several abrasions on her arms and legs. "There are three different peaks to Goose Eye, and they're real slick and will be straight downhill for you in places. And it looks like rain all day tomorrow. They will be REALLY slick."

"We REALLY appreciate the information," I responded, feebly trying not to sound sarcastic.

"Hey, and before you even get to Goose Eye you first have to climb Mt. Success. That's over 1000 feet in elevation gain, in the rain. Man, it's going to be awful. Going down the other side will be worse. I hope you guys can make it. I wouldn't want to be doing that section in a downpour. I'd probably get killed."

I actually wanted to tell the talkative woman with the colorful hair to "shut up," but I somehow maintained my gentlemanly demeanor. What I didn't want to admit was that she was scaring me. Since the beginning of my journey I had tried my utmost to avoid hiking dangerous sections in the rain. From what the would-be soothsayer was describing, the following day's 9.6 miles could prove treacherous. Molar Man, Susquehanna Slim, and Pilgrim had also perked up their ears to the lady's warning.

As the rain's intensity increased, and beginning to be concerned about the potential perilous segment that lay ahead, my buddies and I discussed our options. Molar Man located the Austin Brook Trail on his map. The 3.5 mile trail off of the A.T. led to North Rd. From the road we could get a shuttle or have Sweet Tooth rescue us. We agreed to wait until morning, evaluate the weather, and then make a decision.

Thunder and lightning awakened me more than once as I slept in a shelter for the first time since New York. Hard rain continued at daybreak.

"I think we need to take the side trail to the road," I offered as we watched the steady rain dripping from the eaves of the lean-to. After one night in the woods I was ready for a bed.

It didn't take much convincing for my buddies to agree. Fortunately, we had cell service. Molar Man made a call to Earl at the Cabin, a hostel near Andover, Maine. Earl said he could pick us up at the Austin Brook trailhead on North Rd. Not knowing the conditions of the trail, or how difficult the terrain might be, we had no idea how long the hike would take. Earl estimated our time and told us he would be there at 10:00.

So I began day 140 on a trail that wasn't even the Appalachian Trail. The 3.5 miles we would walk today wouldn't count. Like all the side trails that lead to shelters, or to overlooks with views, these miles were extra. It didn't really matter. I was headed to a dry hostel and a bunk. The hostel was near a small town with at least one restaurant, according to *The A.T. Guide*. After my night in the woods, I would again have the luxury (if that's an appropriate word for a hostel) of a bed and town food. This hiker had no complaints as my companions and I stepped from the Gentian Pond shelter into what had only become a light drizzle.

From the outset this "side trail" appeared to be no different from the A.T. in terms of difficulty. After about a mile, however, the moderate rain was reduced to a sprinkle and the trail leveled substantially. Other than having to wade through some overflowing streams, we made our way to North Rd. in less than two hours, arriving before our ride.

With thunder roaring in the distance, Pilgrim observed, "We're going to get drenched if he doesn't get here soon. I'm getting tired of all this damn rain."

As if to validate the elder member of our group's prophesy, Earl drove up in yet another small car just as (to use a southern axiom) "the bottom fell out." If our new friend from the Cabin had been even thirty seconds later, we assuredly would have again been soaked. The rain commenced in torrents, making it difficult for our driver to see even with his windshield wipers moving on the fast setting.

"Man, I'm glad we're not trying to hike those wet granite slabs in these conditions," I stated somewhat prayerfully. I think everyone felt the same.

Earl and his wife, Marge, have owned the Cabin for several years and even though in their 70's still hike as often as they can as Honey and Bear. On the drive to the hostel, Earl filled us in on some of the sections of trail in western Maine. He seemed to quickly pick up on my apprehension of what lay ahead.

"You have all made it this far; you'll be fine the rest of the way," our new friend reassuringly stated.

He seemed sincere. I took an immediate liking to the grisly, gray-bearded "bear" of a man. I also felt at peace knowing that my buddies and I could use the Cabin as a base camp for the next several days and would benefit from Earl's knowledge of the area.

The rain had practically ceased when we arrived at the place Earl and Marge called home. With a smile that matched her husband's, Marge showed us the bunkhouse and provided each of us with fresh linens. Slim, Pilgrim, and I were assigned the only three bunks remaining in the eight-bed room. Molar Man and Sweet Tooth took the one available private room in the main home.

After taking hot showers and starting a load of laundry, the five of us made our way into downtown Andover. With a population hovering around 800, the quaint New England town offered only three places to dine along S. Main Street. We picked the Little Red Hen. The outstanding hospitality and delicious food took my mind away from wet roots and slippery rocks on the Appalachian Trail. The return of hard rain couldn't detract from my satisfaction with the large slice of blueberry pie I selected for dessert.

Later in the evening we all enjoyed a family-style supper prepared by Marge. Other thru-hikers joined us at the rectangular wooden table. Barbequed chicken legs, corn on the cob, potatoes, and rolls comprised the menu. Large dishes of ice cream followed. Having consumed two huge meals in the past five hours, I figured the day had probably been one in which I had gained weight.

I didn't linger long in the common area of the bunkhouse. A few of the young hikers watched an action movie which I didn't recognize. Another sorted laundry. I deemed a good night's sleep more important. Molar Man wanted to start tomorrow at 3:30. Slim, Pilgrim, and I thought his plan a bit insane. But he and Sweet Tooth had the car, so we acquiesced. I set the alarm and once again lay my head on a pillow to conclude another day on my A.T. journey.

CHAPTER 15

Sleeping Snuggly in Rugged Maine

I got a call from Joe from the Appalachian Trail in July, 2013. He had been on the AT since March. It had been a hard trip—with two serious bouts of Norovirus. He was carrying his food, tent, and necessary items to camp all the way from Georgia to Maine. I met him in the Shenandoah National Park in May and was frightened by how thin and tired he appeared.
It occurred to me then that he might not be able to complete the entire trail—a thought that had never crossed my mind before that week in May.

I was both surprised and relieved when he told me about his new plan. Joe realized that he had lost too much weight and would not be able to finish with Plan A. His Plan B was to join up with Don's Brother and use his method—or the DBM as Joe called it—to get him through the final month or two of the trail. I needed for him to clarify for me exactly what the DBM was. Joe explained that it was doing all of the hiking, but spending as many nights as possible in town, in hotels, hostels, or inns. This way he would be able to eat a big breakfast and dinner, possibly buy a pre-made lunch, and not have to carry a tent, several days of food, cooking equipment, or a sleeping bag. It sounded like a great plan to me. I had been worried about Joe's health. I was sure—and Joe was too—that he would be able to finish the trail using the Don's Brother Method.

Joe hiked with DB and two other guys for a month more. Unfortunately, with only 265 miles left to complete the entire trail in one year, his body quit, and his health required him to return home. Fortunately, in 2015, nearly two years later, he returned to the trail, starting where he had left off in 2013. This time, he decided from the get-go that he was definitely using the DBM, and I was going to be the shuttler. We were fortunate to meet up with a section-hiker that both Joe and DB had met in 2013, Speck, the very first night. Joe joined Speck's group, and I was able to help ease some of the burden of Speck, Wandering One, Still Thinking, and Poego by shuttling their gear from place to place, doing errands in town, getting sandwiches and sodas, and generally doing whatever I could do to make it a little easier for them on their way to Katahdin. Joe finished in August! We made some lifelong friends along the way, and even I had some great adventures while driving through Maine. The Don's Brother Method was a wonderful way to end the adventure.

JOYCE "MOTHER TERESA" ESTES (WEST HILLS, CA)

I IMAGINE THE OTHER HIKERS in the bunkhouse of the Cabin also thought us a bit crazy as we prepared our packs a good two hours before daylight. No one grumbled, although a couple had obviously been awakened. Insinuating that we needed substantial nourishment to hoist our full packs on what might be a grueling day, Molar Man's plan called for a drive all the way back to McDonald's in Gorham for breakfast. Again, no complaints from me. I didn't mind forfeiting the two hours of sleep for hotcakes, sausage, and coffee. Day 141 definitely would go down as the earliest I would arise.

This 141st day on the A.T. would also be recorded as the one which required the longest walk back to the trail. Molar Man seemed to be using his engineering background rather than his dental training when he calculated our start from the Cabin. By the time we had driven to Gorham, eaten our meal, driven to North Rd., hiked the 3.5 mile Austin Brook Trail to the Gentian Pond shelter and the 0.2 mile trail from the shelter to the Appalachian Trail, it was exactly 7:48, or four hours and eighteen minutes since my watch had alarmed. It was going to be a long day.

Carrying full packs in order to spend another night in the woods, my three buddies and I embarked on a day which included ascents and descents of Mt. Success, Mt. Carlo, and the west, east, and north peaks of Goose Eye Mountain. I hated to admit it, but our loud shelter-mate from two nights earlier had been right. This stretch of trail was treacherous. I would definitely have hated to be doing it yesterday in the rain.

When we did occasionally find ourselves walking on an almost flat surface, black mud dominated the trail. At one point both Slim and I found ourselves almost knee-deep in the oozy substance.

"There must be a wooly mammoth down there somewhere," Slim quipped.

Fortunately our gang reached the Full Goose Shelter well before dark. I staked out a spot next to the right wall of the structure and went ahead and blew up my mattress. A little later Pilgrim decided to do the same. Not having felt well for the past few days, my good buddy couldn't seem to accomplish the task. Molar Man, Slim, and I were alarmed at his inability to perform the simple undertaking. Despite eating much better over the past month, Pilgrim's strength continued to decline.

Many other thru-hikers arrived as sundown approached. Southbounders offered information about the Mahoosuc Notch, a section of trail we northbounders would encounter the following morning. Labeled by many as the most difficult mile on the entire A.T., the actual 1.3 mile segment resembles a giant boulder field with oftentimes more than one route to get from point A to point B. Slim had hiked the section previously with his sons. Even though he had said it had been a lot of fun, I still prepared myself mentally for the challenge that lay ahead. With gigantic rocks on my mind, I slept somewhat restlessly on another chilly night.

Before sunrise I heard Molar Man readying his pack. I followed suit, trying to think more about Marge's supper and a bunk at the Cabin than about car-sized rocks. With plans to spend three more nights in the friendly hostel, I also smiled at the thought of two hot meals a day.

But for the moment fantasies of beds and town food needed to be stashed away. My mind would be occupied with surviving the Mahoosuc Notch, the Mahoosuc Arm, and Old Speck Mountain on day 142. And I did. In fact, with the company of my three hiking buddies the first part of the day's adventure actually did contain a few moments of fun. Slim compared the Notch to jungle gyms of childhood. Fortunately, none of us had any falls as we "played" through the mazelike rock masses.

Trepidation still far outweighed glee on one of my hardest days by far. After meticulously winding our way through the Notch, we were faced with the equal difficulty of the Mahoosuc Arm. Then the climb and descent of Old Speck posed another challenge. By the time we reached Grafton Notch we were all exhausted.

Not having pre-arranged a time to be picked up, we had to wait over an hour for Sweet Tooth's arrival. By the time we got back to the Cabin the evening meal had already been concluded. Thankfully, Honey had saved the four of us some supper which she served in the smaller family dining room. Leftovers never tasted so good.

My first full day on the trail in Maine had been eventful. The purported most difficult mile on the A.T. lay behind me. Old Speck was also history. According to Bear, tomorrow's trail would be much more agreeable. So again as day 142 came to a close, I had survived a dangerous section, eaten a delicious hot meal, and was about to sleep with my head on a pillow in a bed. It wasn't the most comfortable of accommodations, but I wasn't in the woods.

Day 143 began at the General Store and Diner in Andover, Maine. Over the next four days, Molar Man, Sweet Tooth, Susquehanna Slim, and I would almost become "regulars." Sitting side by side at the lunch counter with my companions, I perused a menu that offered just about any breakfast item imaginable. Even though hikers are common in the small New England town, we still garnered a few stares from the locals.

A friendly young lady, who seemed much too pleasant for such an early hour, took our orders. I selected scrambled eggs, sausage, toast, and coffee. Slim duplicated my meal, but added oatmeal. We all also bought sandwiches and other snacks for lunch on the trail. We each added a bottle of Gatorade as well.

One of the things that especially makes the Don's Brother Method so convenient is hydration. On most days I left town with an energy drink or two and at least two liters of water from a faucet. The content may sound heavy,

The Don's Brother Method

but as the day progresses, the weight diminishes. Rarely did I need to treat water. I didn't carry a filter, and I only bought Aqua-Mira twice—once before beginning on Springer and again in Harper's Ferry.

With full stomachs and slackpacks for the first time in over a week, Molar Man, Slim, and I hoped that Earl's description of today's hike would be accurate. It was spot on. Other than a few muddy sections, the only real challenge (if it could even be categorized as such) occurred at the west and east peaks of Baldpate. With no rain the past two days, the only slightly slanted rock faces seemed much less imposing than Old Speck had yesterday.

My buddies and I covered the 10.3 miles to East B Hill Rd. by early afternoon. Sweet Tooth was already waiting for the drive back to the Cabin. Plenty of time remained before supper. After the always invigorating hot shower, I lounged outside to write. A cool breeze seemed to be a harbinger of autumn. I could have reminded myself that it was August and probably in the high 90's back in Georgia. But I tried not to.

Before going back inside I spent some time perusing *The A.T. Guide*. I noticed the stars that I had drawn in blue ink along the margins of Maine pages. Each designated either a road or water crossing. The roads represented an escape of sorts, an outlet to safety. Despite being in the most remote state on the trail, there were many. I had marked forty-four. The final twelve occurred in the 100 Mile Wilderness, well over a week in the future. Still, I took solace knowing that if there were a route to a bed, Molar Man and Sweet Tooth would figure out how to find it.

With that thought in mind, I sauntered back inside to join the others for supper. Honey had prepared burgers with all the trimmings. We all tried to enjoy the food; however, a bit of sadness overshadowed the meal. Today had been a somber one.

Having little energy over the past few days, and beginning to lose weight again, Pilgrim determined that it was time to see a doctor. Receiving a diagnosis of Lyme disease, it appeared that the Californian's hike was over. I remembered the first time I had met Pilgrim back in Virginia and how he and Banzai had come to appreciate the Don's Brother Method. I also recalled Pilgrim's shortening my trail name to DB. We would all miss him.

Like the previous morning, our smaller group began day 144 at the Andover General Store and Diner. A different waitress greeted us, also surprisingly cheerful just past sunup. I duplicated yesterday's breakfast, but changed my lunch order from a turkey sandwich to ham. I also bought some snacks, including an Almond Joy, Molar Man's favorite candy. I've recently made it a practice to offer the chocolate-covered coconut treat to my good buddy to lift his spirits. Sweet Tooth also sometimes puts one in his pack, but it's always the snack size. The larger bar makes him smile.

With rain again forecast for the afternoon, my companions and I knew we would be in a race to finish today's hike before it arrived. So at just past 7:00 we headed up the A.T. from East B Hill Rd. The trail ascended at once, with the first climb of the day culminating at Surplus Pond, one of many picturesque lakes we would encounter over the next two weeks. The lakes, or "fishing holes" as my dad would have called them, always reminded me of my brother.

The day passed quickly. We took a break at the Hall Mountain Lean-to for lunch and then walked steadily throughout the early afternoon in a light sprinkle. Still, we reached South Arm Rd. before any significant precipitation. Sweet Tooth stood by the white Volvo ready to whisk us back to the Cabin.

Returning to the dry and warm hostel felt great. I had eaten well and slept comfortably here for three of the past four nights. Our plan called for us to remain for two more. Walking up the stairs to the main home for supper, I felt grateful. I had good folks with whom to share the trail, places to meet new friends and eat and sleep, and a support person for transport to and from the trail each day. All was good, indeed.

A look of surprise appeared on the face of the waitress at the Andover General Store and Diner as our gang took seats at the lunch counter for the third consecutive day. Probably perplexed and quite possibly feeling as if she were experiencing a touch of Deja vu, she nevertheless greeted us with a smile and hot cups of coffee. We also got the glares from the regular patrons, but they would always return a smile when offered one. I think we all felt accepted among the western Mainers.

On this day 145 of my hike from Georgia, I chose to begin my day with hotcakes for a change. Adding a side of bacon, I could not have been more satisfied as I relaxed my feet on a plastic red milk crate foot stool. Even with a more challenging hiking day about to unfold, I was at peace, at least for the moment.

It seems to be becoming a regularity that Molar Man, Slim, and I begin our day on the Appalachian Trail just past 7:00. Today was no exception. At 7:07 to be exact, we immediately were confronted with a 2000 foot elevation gain on the ascent of Old Blue. Over the following two hours, we would descend and then climb another 500 feet to the peak of Bemis Mountain. From the crest the trail actually "leveled" for a few miles.

The 13.2 mile day concluded with one final uphill section, ending at ME 17. We quickly walked up the highway to where Sweet Tooth had parked the Volvo at an overlook with a picturesque view of Lake Mooselookmeguntit. From there it was back to Andover.

Plenty of daylight remained for me to again relax outside to write. After almost a week at the home of Earl and Marge, it would seem strange not returning after tonight. My buddies and I all showed our gratitude to our hosts over one final family-style meal. We all laughed, noting that we had stayed so long at the hostel that the menu had repeated itself.

Driving away from the Cabin for a final time on the morning of day 146, I couldn't help but think about how fortunate I was to have met these two fine people. I also thought about all the thru-hikers who walk the Appalachian Trail every year without taking the time to visit small communities like Andover. After all, Andover isn't actually on the trail. It's a pretty long commute from Grafton Notch and even longer from where we first shuttled in from North Rd. Some hikers do come in from East B Hill Rd. or South Arm Rd., (8.0 miles east and 9.0 miles east of the trail respectively); however, many hikers probably just pass on by without ever having the opportunity to meet Earl and Marge or without enjoying breakfast at the Andover General Store and Diner.

As I resumed my walk through the 14th state of the A.T., I continued to be thankful that I had hiked in this manner. The Cabin had reinforced my belief in the Don's Brother Method. I would keep hiking every step north toward Katahdin, but I would also do my best to visit each town along the way that lies remotely close to the Appalachian Trail. There is much peace and solitude in the woods. But there are wonderful people to be met and places to eat in the cities and towns along the way.

And speaking of eating, we couldn't depart from Andover without one final country breakfast at the General Store. We arrived just as it opened at 5:00. After having become almost a "regular" over the past week, I remarked to the store's owner that this would be our last day in the area. He thanked us for our patronage and wished us well with the remainder of our hike. So after another delicious meal, we headed back to ME 17 to resume our journey.

The 13.2 miles of the trail today proved to be about as "easy" as any I've encountered since Vermont. The occasional occurrence of mud prompted another of Slim's "wooly mammoth" references. With almost no elevation gains to speak of, I could deal with the small patches of the black, squishy substance. Knowing that I had a new pair of trail runners waiting at the post office in Rangeley, I made no effort to keep this pair that had served me well since Wingdale, New York, clean.

When our group reached ME 4, Sweet Tooth was again waiting in a parking area adjacent to the trail. We made a brief stop for gas and some groceries before heading to the Town and Lake Motel. Rather than getting two rooms, we decided to share a two bedroom cabin. After checking in, Slim and I walked a couple of blocks to town center. My buddy from New Jersey got a haircut. I bought new socks and treated myself to an ice cream cone. I also picked up my package before strolling back to the motel.

Later in the evening we dined at the Shed, a barbecue place with inside picnic table seating. Although not as tasty as what I was accustomed to in the south, I've yet to complain about town food on this thru-hike of the Appalachian Trail. As I thought about it, I remembered other barbecue meals in Tennessee, Virginia, and New York. We planned the next few days over our ribs and pulled-pork.

The dining experience underwent a change on the morning of day 147. With a kitchen at our disposal, and seeing an opportunity to save a few dollars,

Sweet Tooth proposed that she cook our breakfast. Molar Man, Slim, and I happily accepted her offer. We shared a dozen eggs, a pound of bacon, and almost half a loaf of bread before making our way back to ME 4.

With over 23 miles between ME 4 and the next navigable road, the gang had reluctantly determined that a night in a shelter would be necessary. There are two marked "woods roads" listed in *The A.T. Guide*; however, neither looked even remotely accessible by car. So as my buddies and I headed up the trail a little after 6:00, our destination for the day was the Poplar Ridge Lean-to.

Today's 10.7 mile hike contained three significant climbs including two 4000 footers, Saddleback Mountain and the Horn. They were followed by only slightly smaller Saddleback Junior. Even though the sheer rock faces required slow movement on my part, the views were well worth the deliberation. We found ourselves at the shelter around 2:00, leaving lots of idle time before bedtime. Later, a light rain began as I settled into my sleeping bag at dusk.

Comparable to the few other days when I had spent a night in the woods, I awoke before dawn. Most A.T. thru-hikers anticipate "town days" with excitement. Our shelter mates on this cold, damp morning were no exception. For me, however, almost every day is a town day. With only a little over a fortnight remaining on my walk toward Katahdin, I had only spent consecutive nights in the woods three times.

Regardless of what might have been, I began day 148 with treating a bottle of water, something I rarely do. It is always more convenient to fill water bottles from spigots or faucets when in town. Today I didn't have that luxury. Nor did I have a hot breakfast. The two pop tarts would have to suffice. So with less than a full stomach, I joined Molar Man and Slim for a 6:20 departure from camp. With a scheduled 13.2 mile section, we hoped to reach our ending point by mid-afternoon.

From the outset my patience was tested. We were greeted by a rather precipitous segment of trail within the first mile. After successfully making my way down the very steep and slick rock slabs, I faced ascents of Spaulding and later Sugarloaf Mountain. The final two miles descended almost 2000 feet to

Caribou Valley Rd. Since the pothole-filled gravel road was not accessible near the A.T. crossing, my buddies and I still needed to walk about one-half mile up the road to where our ever-reliable driver stood alongside the white Volvo.

The rickety ride to the main road required slow driving; however, once off the gravel, we quickly made our way to Stratton. Similar to Andover, the small town of Stratton provided everything our party would need for the next three nights. Having reserved two of the five rooms at the Stratton Motel, we checked in and arranged to do laundry. The combination motel/hostel offers the bare minimum, but it does sit next to the White Wolf Inn. The Inn's eating establishment would become our restaurant of choice during the stay in Stratton.

I began day 149 with a breakfast sandwich from the Northland Cash Supply, located on Main St. just a few yards from the motel. Even though we only had a short 9.1 mile day planned, Molar Man still insisted that we start early. Since of course he had the car, Slim and I agreed. Clutching a second cup of coffee, I sat quietly in the back seat on the ride back to Caribou Valley Rd.

Continuing to cling to my now only luke-warm beverage on the walk up the gravel road back to the A.T., I lagged behind my companions before we had even begun the hike. When we did reach the trail, we were immediately confronted with South Crocker Mountain. The almost 2000 foot ascent over only two miles left me a little winded. Still, the terrain for the most part was agreeable. North Crocker followed with an additional 200 foot elevation gain.

For the remainder of the short, less than five hours day, the trail descended. The three of us reached ME 27 around noon. Sweet Tooth was already waiting. We paused for a short lunch, left our packs with our driver, and then walked a remarkably flat 0.8 stretch of trail to Stratton Brook Pond Rd. It's always nice to go packless, even for a short time. Moving at a rapid pace, our band of three reached the stopping point for the day before Sweet Tooth. When she did arrive, we headed back to Stratton.

After hot showers, Susquehanna Slim and I moseyed over to the White Wolf for a second lunch. Knowing that I would eat again in a few hours, I only selected a large burger and fries.

The Don's Brother Method

"I wonder how many different restaurants I've eaten in on my thru-hike," I remarked to Slim.

"Probably more than you would have eaten in at home," my friend noted with a smile.

No doubt he was right. Sometimes I felt just a little guilty with the Don's Brother Method. Then I reminded myself that the difficulty of the trail didn't alter, no matter where one took his meals or slept at night. I also noted that rarely did I go into a restaurant remotely close to the A.T. without seeing another hiker dining as well. And all the rooms at the Stratton Motel and the bunks at the hostel were full tonight---with Appalachian Trail thru-hikers.

Throughout the rest of the afternoon I lounged on the front porch of the room I shared with Slim. Across the street shoppers occasionally arrived to enter Fotter's Market. At the far end of the small hostel other hikers visited at picnic tables. Not recognizing any of the group, I decided to meander on over and introduce myself.

"I'm Don's Brother; are all of you thru-hiking?" By the looks on their haggard faces, and by the gear that lay on the ground around the table, I realized the absurdity of my question. None of the young folks responded inappropriately. "When did you start?" I continued.

Most had begun their hikes after me and obviously were moving at a quicker pace. One, however, had started the same week as I.

"It just seems so odd that we've been hiking the same trail for nearly five months and are meeting for the first time," I noted to Red Knees.

"We have met before. Back in Georgia, I think," the youngster responded.

The young man was right. Upon checking my journal, I discovered that Red Knees and I had met previously, but it was near Max Patch in North Carolina. It felt good to be remembered.

The following morning Slim and I ordered lunch sandwiches from the deli at Fotter's for the long day ahead. I also doubled my usual Gatorade allotment, anticipating a warmer day than usual as well. Even though Stratton is small, between the White Wolf, Fotter's, and the Northland Cash Supply, good town food was abundant.

Day 150 called for the greatest distance since that hellacious day on Kinsman Mountain in the Whites. It would also be one of the most scenic of my entire hike. The 16.1 miles my buddies and I travelled today consisted of the Bigelow Range which includes Avery Peak, the 2000 mile mark from Springer and the last 4000 footer before Katahdin. On a gorgeous sunny August afternoon, we lingered at the summit, just enjoying.

The miles sped by, bringing us to Bog Brook Rd. before 5:00. As always, Sweet Tooth was waiting. We made our way back to Stratton for one more night at the Stratton Motel. I continued to be enormously grateful to be provided this full-time support.

For a third consecutive night, Slim and I dined at the White Wolf. As we were being seated, we passed two hikers at a window booth.

"Hey, Don's Brother," one voiced with surprise. When the gentleman realized that I wasn't recognizing him, he continued, "I'm Army Ant."

The last time I saw the recent retiree from Rhode Island was in Georgia. Like I noted yesterday to Red Knees, "It's amazing how we have been hiking the same trail for five months and haven't seen each other for over 1900 miles."

"Such is life on the A.T.," Army Ant replied.

We each shared a little about our hikes while waiting for our meals.

As it was with other "base camps" that had served me well going all the way back to Erwin, Tennessee, it was going to be hard leaving Stratton. This motel, like so many others in trail towns, would be one where a hiker probably would never stay if he were not "a hiker." Still, they provide beds with pillows and indoor plumbing and are usually in proximity to town food. I had slept well and eaten well in Stratton. Tomorrow would take Molar Man, Slim, and me back to the woods. On second thought, with good friends around, I didn't mind the change.

My buddies and I began day 151 like the previous two with a stroll across the road to Fotter's Market. Again, I purchased a breakfast sandwich and a twelve inch sub for lunch in the woods. I also added some snacks and my daily bottle of Gatorade.

From Stratton we drove back to Bog Brook Rd. where yesterday's hike had concluded. Just past 7:00 we hit the trail. Today's plan called for Sweet

Tooth to drive some backwoods roads to the Harrison Pierce Pond Camps, where we would meet her for the night. Even with a GPS, maps, and phone directions from the Camp's owner, Tim, poor Sweet Tooth experienced some difficulties. Apparently the roads were easier to navigate with a four-wheel drive pick-up than with a Volvo station wagon. Tim would later tell us that in winter he could only get out by snowmobile.

Still able to carry slackpacks, and walking on relatively flat terrain all day, we made incredibly good time. Even with several stops to admire the many lakes in the region, we arrived at our destination before 3:00. The 16.5 miles had zipped by.

The Camps consist of a large main structure with a dining room, kitchen, and common area which houses a pool table. A wraparound porch also afforded us the opportunity to witness the activity of literally dozens of hummingbirds that were drawn to the numerous feeders hung on the eaves. Molar Man, Sweet Tooth, Slim, and I each selected from the eclectic assortment of chairs to rest. Cabins fronting a fast-running brook are also available for overnight stays. Slim and I shared one and Molar Man and Sweet Tooth took another. There is also a bathhouse with a shower. The running water works off of a generator.

After dining on the remainder of my lunch sandwich, I challenged Slim to a game of pool. Later Tim joined us with a glass of wine. He shared some stories and I did as well. Once again I felt fortunate to get to know another of the many good people who reside near the Appalachian Trail.

The following morning I was treated to a beyond-outstanding breakfast. Tim is known for his world-class pancakes. The traditional serving is 12. I opted for the half order, along with sausage, eggs, juice, and coffee. Many hikers who camp nearby, or stay in the Pierce Pond Lean-to, still stop in for breakfast. Reservations are appreciated since Tim does all the cooking. On this, my 152st day on the A.T., Tim served in two shifts. Our group was in the first at 7:00.

The early start was mandated by the crossing of the Kennebec River, 3.2 miles north of the Camps. The Kennebec is the only water crossing on the Appalachian Trail where fording is prohibited. A ferryman provides transport over the potentially dangerous river. His canoe even sports a white blaze on its bottom. The service is only available between 9 and 11 AM and 2 and 4 PM. We wanted to ensure that we reached the crossing as early as possible in case other hikers were waiting.

When we arrived at the river, we discovered that a pair had beaten us to the mark. Still, the wait was brief. Since only two are allowed in the canoe with the ferryman, Slim and I rode together. Molar Man followed with thru-hiker, Torch. On the northern bank of the river a pack of Boy Scouts prepared for a southern crossing.

0.3 miles after the Kennebec, we reached US 201 where Sweet Tooth waited with a cooler of cold drinks. She always offered beverages and snacks to other hikers passing by as well. Three were enjoying her kindness when we reached the road.

From the highway, my companions and I continued to experience rather flat segments of trail all the way to Pleasant Pond Rd. Molar Man and I planned to conclude a comfortably short 8.8 mile day there. Susquehanna Slim, however, had decided otherwise.

Needing to reach Katahdin more quickly than Molar Man and I did, Slim wanted to cover more miles over the next few days than we were scheduling. He also needed to return to Vermont and complete a section of trail that he had omitted. Molar Man and I were both sorry to see Slim leave, but we understood his situation. I felt a little sad watching him walk up the trail and out of my hike.

Slim would be back in the woods tonight. A part of me wanted to join him, at least for a moment. Our plans, however, called for a night at the Sterling Inn near Caratunk. The recently re-opened B & B offers rooms to hikers at reasonable rates, has some minimal re-supply items, and provides breakfast. Unfortunately, we would only be able to stay for one night.

Shortly after checking in, Molar Man, Sweet Tooth, and I travelled into nearby Bingham where we enjoyed lunch at Thompson's Restaurant. I doubt if many thru-hikers ever frequent this quaint town or meet the wonderful folks at Thompson's. Before leaving I treated myself to a homemade Whoopie Pie for dessert.

After lunch we drove into Monson, the last significant town prior to the 100 Mile Wilderness. We needed to do some reconnaissance work in preparation for the final major stretch of trail before Baxter State Park and Katahdin. I had heard of a few others who had managed to slackpack the Wilderness. Molar Man and I wanted to investigate just how it could be done.

We first stopped by the 100 Mile Wilderness Adventures and Outfitters to speak with Phil. Providing shuttles for hikers who want or need to exit this remote section of trail, Phil offered us information about roads that are navigable as well as warnings about which roads to avoid. We listened and learned. And we greatly appreciated Phil's sharing his knowledge with us.

For the remainder of the day I relaxed at the Sterling Inn, dividing my time between the front porch, the upstairs TV room, the downstairs parlor, and my comfortable bedroom. My thoughts returned to the trail and the major challenges it poses all hikers. The towns along the way, however, can provide a needed respite for any who choose to indulge.

With no suitable roads from which to escape the trail over the next 30 or so miles, Molar Man and I resigned ourselves to another night in the woods. Two gravel roads intersect the trail just past the lean-to where we planned to spend the night; however, Phil discouraged us from attempting to use either of these.

So on the morning of day 153 Molar Man and I ventured back into the woods, carrying full packs. For the first time since Pennsylvania, there would just be the two of us today. My mind wandered back to our first meeting in the Smokies. Molar Man had been my first steady hiking partner on this journey, and now it appeared that he would be the last. That was fine with me, and I expected he felt the same.

Having only one significant ascent on the day's agenda, Pleasant Pond Mountain, at 2:00 my buddy and I reached our stopping place for the evening. We discussed briefly moving on to the next lean-to. But since we had no tents, we didn't think it wise to hike the additional 8.9 miles with the possibility that the shelter would be filled. In hindsight, we probably could have managed to make it all the way to a paved Shirley-Blanchard Rd. where Sweet Tooth could have met us. That would have given us a 25.2 mile day, a distance we hadn't covered in a while, and perhaps too far considering the terrain.

Actually, our decision to stop for the night at Moxie Bald Mountain Lean-to was a good one. As close as we were to Katahdin, there was really no reason to jeopardize our hike with a longer than usual distance. After that initial climb, the terrain posed only a few challenges, but we hadn't known that would be the case when we planned the day.

When we arrived at the shelter two weekenders had already taken up about half of the space. I placed my mattress next to the right wall. Molar Man selected a spot near the center. Later in the afternoon four more hikers arrived, forcing all of us to move a little nearer to each other in the 8-person lean-to.

Despite close quarters, I slept reasonably well in the woods. I awoke to chirping birds at dawn. Other than Molar Man, no one was yet stirring. In fact, when we headed up the trail at 6:20 everyone else in the shelter still appeared to be sleeping. I hoped that my minimal cold breakfast of two cereal bars would not reduce my energy level. Another town was our destination as I began day 154.

The Appalachian Trail in Maine presents more water crossings than any of its other thirteen states. Few bridges are constructed here due to potential high maintenance caused by melting snow. Thus, many of these rivers, streams, and brooks require fording. Today we would encounter six of them. On three occasions Molar Man and I removed our hiking shoes and replaced them with camp shoes to walk through the water. Fortunately, none were very deep. With little rain over the past few days, each time the water level only reached mid-calf.

After making our way across the East Branch of the Piscataquis River, we sat on a couple of large rocks to have lunch. Knowing that a hot meal awaited later that evening, I didn't really mind the cold food. Since I rarely carried a full pack, and since I seldom spent more than one night on the trail, I often brought along a couple of canned items. Today I dined on my favorite: Beanie Weenies.

Feeling somewhat lethargic, we slowed our pace in the afternoon. Luckily, the final 6.7 miles of the 17.9 mile day presented no real problems. Other than one uneventful 200 foot elevation gain, the trail was remarkably flat. Before

The Don's Brother Method

4:00 we arrived at ME 15. It felt good to see Sweet Tooth and the white Volvo. I was definitely ready for a shower.

Even though we were only four miles from Monson and a hostel, the three of us decided to head on up the road an additional ten miles to Greenville. A slightly larger town, Greenville offered a better selection of motels, an outfitter, and a supermarket. In order to save on expenses, we chose to share a two bedroom efficiency at the Moosehead Lakefront Motel. To further save, Sweet Tooth prepared supper.

Later in the evening I reclined in an Adirondack chair on a grassy bank overlooking Moosehead Lake. Thinking about all the thru-hikers who had made their way from Georgia to Maine over the years, I wondered how many had stayed here. I doubted that many had. Without the support of Molar Man and Sweet Tooth, I probably wouldn't be here either. On this cool, late August night, I continued to be grateful for this opportunity to "hike my own hike." Tomorrow we would take one final day off to plan the final ten days of our adventure on the Appalachian Trail.

With the Don's Brother Method, or as I felt it should be called at times, the Molar Man Method, long-range planning is essential. So we set aside day 155 for scouting. If we were going to slackpack the 100 Mile Wilderness successfully, we needed to be certain where the roads were that Sweet Tooth would use to get us in and then get us out each day.

The section of trail from ME 15, near Monson, to Golden Rd., 19 miles east of Millinocket, is referred to as the 100 Mile Wilderness for a reason. The A.T. crosses no main highways or roads for 99.1 miles, to be exact. There are also no towns along this isolated stretch. There are gravel and rutted roads, however, which provide access to this segment of trail. But it can prove difficult to locate and figure out how to get to these roads and to determine exactly where these roads intersect with the A.T. Even with GPS coordinates, getting lost is definitely a possibility.

On a beautiful sunny morning, which would have been a great day to hike, we instead headed into the Wilderness, by car. Our initial task was to locate Otter Pond Rd., the first drivable road after ME 15 that is actually listed in *The A.T. Guide* as having a parking area. The only problem that the three of us could find was that the so-called "parking area" would have to be accessed from the A.T. via an unmarked 0.8 mile trail just past the Long Pond Stream Lean-to. We found the road and the unblazed trail without too much difficulty. Our only minor concern was that Sweet Tooth could locate it again the following day.

After a stop at a country store for lunch, our next destination was the first of two gated logging roads that may be used to access the trail, for a fee. Since Katahdin Ironworks Rd. leads to private property, everyone who enters must pay. That is each person, not each car. In 2013 the charge was $12 per person to enter. There is no charge to exit. So on the days that Sweet Tooth would drop Molar Man and me back at the trail, we would all have to pay. The fee was good for the entire day, so Sweet Tooth could depart and return without having to pay again.

From the gate we had little difficulty finding the parking area of the West Branch of the Pleasant River. And from the looks of the parking lot, no one else had either. I shot a little video on my phone of the fast-moving logging trucks. This area certainly didn't look like much of a wilderness. Molar Man and I also walked up a path to where the A.T. crosses. This would be our ending point two days from now.

With only a few hours of sunlight remaining, we drove to the other logging road that leads to the trail, Jo-Mary Rd. Since we had already paid to enter at Katahdin Ironworks Rd. earlier, we were not charged an additional fee. One ticket per day allows access to either road. Even though a little more remote, we still met a few cars as we sought to find A.T. crossings located off of Jo-Mary. It took some time, but old Molar Man found them all.

Feeling confident that our day of reconnaissance had been well worth the time, we headed back to Greenville for another night at the Moosehead Lakefront Motel. Along the way we happened upon the first McDonald's we had seen since Gorham. The Dover-Foxcroft, Maine location looked like any other. We ate our supper, and I purchased burgers for the next day's hike. I figured I'd enjoy my first day in the Wilderness more with Mickey D's for lunch.

At the motel I placed my burgers in the fridge before taking a stroll which led me back to the lake. Enjoying a hot cup of coffee on the chilly night, I lounged in the familiar Adirondack chair and thought about the past five months. The finish line was only a few miles ahead. Looking across the glistening lake, I admitted to myself that I was ready for my adventure to come to an end.

CHAPTER 16

Slackpacking the Wilderness

As a person supporting a thru-hiker, knowing how to get from point A to point B was essential. The most helpful advice came from Honey, who along with her husband, Bear, owned the Cabin near Andover, ME. She told me that a GPS doesn't always work. I had found that to be very true. She suggested using GDS: Guys Down the Street. 'If you wanted to know how to find a trail or road that wasn't marked on the map, just visit the local fast food place in the early morning. There will be several older gentlemen who know the area intimately.' She was right. Whenever we needed such assistance, the GDS worked every time!

DIANE "SWEET TOOTH" EICHELBERGER (SPRINGFIELD, OH)

BACK IN ERWIN, TN, SOME four months earlier, I had met 5:30, a former thru-hiker. Over breakfast at the Super 8, 5:30 explained how he had gotten his trail name. Apparently his alarm had awakened the entire Walasi-Yi bunkhouse at an early hour one morning. Naturally the young folks immediately dubbed the slender, bearded, older gentleman, 5:30.

When I related to 5:30 that I was using Erwin as a base for a few days as I attempted to hike every day, yet return to a room every night, he acknowledged that he had also frequented quite a few towns the previous year.

"I even slackpacked most of the 100 Mile Wilderness," 5:30 kind of boasted.

Already dreading the thought of spending several consecutive nights in the remote woods of Maine, I was anxious to hear how it could be done.

"It's expensive, but there are people who will shuttle you in and out for a price."

So as Molar Man, Sweet Tooth, and I drove back to the trailhead at ME 15, I thought of 5:30. As day 156 began, we were about to see if our slackpacking plan would work.

From its outset, this first day in the Wilderness didn't look any different from other recent days on the trail in Maine. Rocks, roots, rock slabs, mud, ups and downs……yeah, it was the same. Then there was the water. We walked past numerous scenic ponds. Brooks and streams also made several appearances. The trail circumvented some. We rock-hopped a few and forded others. None really posed a problem.

Around noon Molar Man and I found a suitable spot for lunch. I have to admit I felt a little embarrassed when thru-hikers Klutz and Mountain Goat passed as I was unwrapping a McDonald's double cheeseburger. Klutz displayed her pretty smile. Mountain Goat just shook his head in disbelief. I had also brought along a bottled Coca-Cola and some chips. So my first meal on the trail in the Wilderness was fast food. With the Don's Brother Method, it seemed only appropriate.

Throughout the afternoon my energy level diminished. Molar Man seemed to be experiencing fatigue as well. With the almost certainty of rain later in the day, we tried to pick up the pace after fording Big Wilson Stream. Five miles still remained before we would reach our significant landmark, the Long Pond Stream Lean-to. When we saw the sign indicating the blue-blazed trail to the shelter, we knew that the unmarked trail we were looking for would be 0.2 miles farther north.

A few minutes later we stood gazing at what appeared to be our exit route. I'm sure that my buddy and I both experienced a twinge of apprehension as we headed down the side trail. There would be no blazes on this seldom-used path that we desperately hoped would lead to the Otter Pond parking area.

With darkness approaching, we almost elevated our pace to a jog over the 0.8 miles. I definitely felt glad that I had a hiking partner for this venture.

In less than half an hour we emerged from the thick foliage to see the white Volvo. The only vehicle in the grassy field never looked so good. I think that Sweet Tooth was as relieved to see us as we were to be safely at the car.

We didn't linger in this isolated area. Within minutes we were on our way out of the woods to a paved highway which would take us back to Greenville for one final night. We picked up some food for supper along the way before arriving back at the Moosehead Lakefront Motel after dark. Much too tired to spend time by the lake, I updated my journal and then called it a night. Molar Man suggested that we get an early start tomorrow. Reluctantly, I set my watch alarm for 4:30 before almost immediately falling asleep in a most comfortable bed.

Using the Don's Brother Method in the 100 Mile Wilderness requires patience. Getting back to the Otter Pond Parking area took over an hour, not counting a stop at a convenience store for a quick breakfast sandwich. With the early wake-up call, we were still able to reach the trail before 7:00 on day 157. After a good night's rest in town, I didn't mind the 0.8 mile I had to walk to start my day before I could begin counting the miles on the Appalachian Trail.

Planning a 15.0 mile day, Molar Man and I didn't take into consideration the difficulty level of the day's hike. In *The A.T. Guide* this section appears rather non-descript with only minimal elevation changes. That was not to be the case. I stumbled often and fell more than once. Several portions demanded deliberate hiking once again. The descent of Chairback Mountain necessitated that I again sit to inch my way down the treacherous rock slabs. Gratefully, they were not wet.

By the time my buddy and I reached the gravel Katahdin Ironworks Rd., my mood hovered somewhere between agitation and indifference. The trail had bested me today. I wasn't sure whether to be angry or just not to care. All that really concerned me was hiking another 85.9 miles and finishing this miserable trail. The A.T. had definitely become my enemy on this warmer, tiring day.

When Molar Man and I did arrive at a woods road, I barely spoke to Sweet Tooth or to two other thru-hikers who were enjoying some chips and soda. Instead, I dropped my pack and kept walking.

Farther up the trail at the West Branch of the Pleasant River, a level path leads from the A.T. to a parking lot. While we walked the additional one-half mile on the A.T. and up the path, Sweet Tooth drove from the woods road to meet us at the parking lot. The day had thrown some challenges my way, yet I started feeling better on the drive up the gravel road. Once back to ME 11, we still had about a forty minute drive to Milo, and a B & B owned by Everett and Frieda Cook.

Milo is a town that is seldom mentioned in books about the Appalachian Trail. It's doubtful that many thru-hikers have stayed in the hamlet of just over 2000 residents. In fact, it's the only place with a bed that we could find even remotely close to the A.T. between Monson and Millinocket. Then again, most hikers don't exit the Wilderness between those two locations.

After we had all showered and visited briefly with the delightful older couple, Molar Man, Sweet Tooth and I shared a meal at the Milo House of Pizza. Only two other booths were occupied on a lazy Monday night. I also ordered food to take with me on the following day's hike. Once again I would be enjoying town food in the Wilderness.

Back at the Cook's home I reclined in a front porch bench swing to write. Eventually, mosquitoes drove me inside on the rather warm Maine evening. Day 157 had been a tough one. Even though the elevations were never over 2501 feet, I had found myself in precarious predicaments more times than I had expected, especially this late in the hike. Nevertheless, I had eaten well, was clean, and had an extremely comfortable bed in which to spend the night. Overall, how could I possibly have any complaints?

Day 158 started with a delicious meal prepared by Frieda. She and Everett joined Molar Man, Sweet Tooth, and me around the kitchen table. With few towns in the area, and even fewer towns with motels or B & B's, locating a bed can be almost as challenging as reaching the summit of a rocky peak. We were fortunate to have found this comfortable home in Milo. Since Molar Man and I had decided to stay one more night in the woods, Sweet Tooth would be returning alone for another night with the Cooks.

After breakfast we were faced with a lengthy drive back to the A.T. When attempting to slackpack the 100 Mile Wilderness, these commutes are to be expected. It took almost an hour to reach the Katahdin Ironworks Rd. Before continuing up the gravel road, we first had to stop and pay our $12 entry fee. Then almost another half hour awaited before we would reach the trail. Even though we had arisen at 5:00, it was 7:20 before we took our first hiking step of the day.

That first step was a wet one. Returning to the A.T. via a path from the Katahdin Ironworks Rd., today's hike began with a ford. I sat on a rock to exchange my trail runners for my plastic Vivo Barefoot camp shoes to walk across the West Branch of Pleasant River. Thankfully, the water level was low. *The A.T. Guide* warned of a "slick rocky bottom." I crossed with caution, yet never came close to losing my balance. It felt good to begin the day with a smile, even though there would be no bed or hot meal on my agenda tonight.

With only one road over a 21.8 mile stretch, Molar Man and I had determined that a hike of that distance was not wise. The one road, Kokadjo-B Pond, is reachable by vehicle. Considering that we would have to climb and descend Gulf Hagas Mountain and later White Cap, the last significant mountain before Katahdin, we feared that would be just too far to walk. So it was with full packs that we forded the river on a partly cloudy morning.

After confronting some difficult terrain and falling three times, I was definitely tired when we reached the Logan Brook Lean-to early in the afternoon. Knowing that this would likely be my last night in a shelter, I thought about other nights I had stayed in the woods since leaving Springer Mountain. This was only my 19th. Others may have spent fewer nights in the woods during their thru-hikes; however, I felt satisfied with **my** thru-hike and how it had been accomplished.

I slept well, awaking at 5:20. Molar Man was already stuffing his pack. Only a few minutes after 6:00 we headed up the trail. Had we known yesterday how agreeable the hike would be today, I think Molar Man and I would have continued to Kokadjo-B Pond Rd. Other than a mild ascent of Little Broadman Mountain, the trail afforded us smooth sailing all day. In fact, day 159 was one of the "easiest" (dare I use that word) of the entire 164 of my journey.

The Don's Brother Method

The hours and miles zipped by. Covering 11.7 before noon, we stopped at the Cooper Brook Falls Lean-to for lunch. From there, I could have run the final 3.7 miles to Jo-Mary Rd. (that is, had I not been carrying a full pack). When we arrived, Sweet Tooth was again offering cold sodas and snacks to two other hikers. I had to smile thinking about how some must be wondering why this stretch is called the 100 Mile Wilderness.

A short while later Molar Man, Sweet Tooth, and I were back on ME 11 headed to Millinocket, the last town on a northbound thru-hike of the Appalachian Trail. We checked in at the Katahdin Inn, an independent motel which appeared to have been previously part of a major chain. With a spacious lobby, including pool tables and a swimming pool, this looked like a suitable place to use as a base for the next five days. The Inn, located at the end of a strip mall with an IGA, House of Pizza, and Family Dollar, was also within a couple of hundred yards of a McDonald's. A Dunkin Donuts and a Subway stood directly across the highway.

It felt good to settle into my own comfortable room again. I imagined that other thru-hikers had stayed here before; however, I doubted that many had taken up residence with over fifty miles yet to be hiked. I couldn't have been happier. This was the Don's Brother Method at its best.

For the next five days Molar Man and I would follow a fairly rigid routine. We would awake around 5:00 and have breakfast provided at the motel, or pick up something at McDonald's. Sweet Tooth would drive us back to the trail to hike with a slackpack which would contain a sandwich from Subway and a soft drink for lunch. Each day we would travel the pre-determined distance to a road where Sweet Tooth would be waiting. Then it would be back to Millinocket for a hot shower, restaurant meal, and a good night's sleep in a bed. For us, the final 57.7 miles of the 100 Mile Wilderness would border on luxury.

Not having dined at the Golden Arches since Dover-Foxcroft, I thoroughly enjoyed my Big Mac meal on this first night in Millinocket. Being from the south, I also greatly appreciated the sweet tea that is a universal part of the fast food empire's menu. I gazed at the final few pages of *The A.T. Guide* over supper. Looking at the gentle terrain that the trail seemed to be promising over this final stretch, I couldn't stop smiling. It would be a light pack and beds for the remainder of the hike. The miles wouldn't always be "big" because big miles didn't always coincide with road crossings. In this stage of my hike, however, there was no hurry.

At times I just wished my fellow hiker felt the same. With long drives back to the A.T. each day, I suppose I understood Molar Man's mandatory 5:00 wake-up time. We were the first in the small dining area of the motel at the beginning of day 160. Like most days, my now good friend, hiking buddy prepared himself a motel waffle. I had grown tired of the self-made, rubbery carbohydrate three states earlier. Instead, I had cold cereal and a Danish. I placed three more of the sweet, fat-filled pastries in the pockets of my rain jacket before walking to the Volvo.

Noticing puddles in the parking lot from last night's downpour, I wondered how wet we could expect to find the trail. A little over an hour later I would find out. Today may have been the wettest since that hike into Hanover over a month ago. For the better part of the 15.0 mile stretch, we were confronted with water obstacles. Molar Man and I forded or rock-hopped most of the bodies of water. Once, however, our only option was to sit on a blown down tree and shimmy across a swollen stream.

What also made today's hike even more nerve-wracking was not knowing where Sweet Tooth would be waiting. When we had sought information about the Wilderness from Phil back in Monson, he had mentioned an unmarked logging road that he sometimes used for shuttles. Sweet Tooth could access the little-used road from Jo-Mary. We just weren't exactly sure where the A.T. crossed it.

Our original thought had been that the crossing would be near the Nahmakanta Stream Campsite. When we arrived there to find no road, and obviously no Sweet Tooth, it became clear that our day would include an additional three miles. For the most part, those miles were flat. Still, I fell once on an invisible root tucked beneath a patch of black mud. We trudged through a quagmire for over an hour before finally arriving at our rendezvous point.

Regardless of all the water we had to deal with, the 15.0 miles again went quickly. We needed less than seven hours to arrive at a very drivable woods road. I smiled, wondering if another Volvo had ever been here. Again, I think Molar Man and I both felt a tinge of relief, after a day of uncertainty and not fully aware of where our ride back to civilization would be located in the Wilderness.

Before heading to Millinocket, we first diverted our route from ME 11 to Golden Road. Abol Bridge would be our stopping point day after tomorrow, so we wanted to make sure Sweet Tooth knew how to get there. We also stopped by the Ranger Station in Baxter State Park to check on parking regulations. Since only a certain number of slots are available adjacent to the campground, we needed to secure the necessary reservation.

While Molar Man and Sweet Tooth spoke with a ranger, I moseyed over to a replica of Katahdin. Staring at the monolith with noticeable facial apprehension, I heard the voice of one of the rangers.

"When you get to the really hard part, there is rebar to use for climbing. There are only a few dangerous places. Hikers rarely get seriously injured, but the weather can be unpredictable."

I wasn't sure whether the uniformed gentleman was trying to ameliorate my fears or just having a little fun with someone whose countenance obviously revealed anxiety. Whatever his intentions, he wasn't in any way making me feel better about climbing to the summit of the prodigious mountain. In no way was he alleviating my uneasiness. The comments didn't seem to be affecting Molar Man, but I listened.

On the drive back to Millinocket I continued to feel anxious. I had hiked over 2100 miles, endured scores of obstacles along the way, and experienced numerous harrowing experiences. So why was I so fearful of this final climb, I wondered. Like the other challenges that I had confronted over the past five months, I would just have to deal with whatever the trail had to throw at me. After all, it was only another mountain.

Back at the Katahdin Inn I took advantage of the onsite laundry. I don't know which felt better……the hot shower, the clean clothes, or the restaurant meal. A three-way tie seemed most appropriate. With only four days remaining, and Katahdin on my mind, I took comfort in knowing that the room I was sitting in would be my home until summit day.

The following morning began like the previous one. A 5:00 alarm awakened me. I choked down one of Molar Man's favorite waffles at the motel and again took along a couple of Danishes. Clouds greeted us as we tossed our packs into the back of the Volvo. I took advantage of the dreary morning to nap on the way back to the A.T.

Our schedule for day 161 called for only 8.7 miles from the unmarked logging road off of Jo-Mary Rd. to another obscure outlet near Pollywog Stream. With GPS coordinates in *The A.T. Guide* indicating a parking area, this meeting point wouldn't be as challenging to locate. Since Molar Man and I expected to be finished with the day's hike before noon, Sweet Tooth decided to remain in the Wilderness. A lover of books, our support driver has gone through quite a library since February. Today she would sit, read, and wait.

Other than one 700 foot ascent of Nesuntabunt Mountain, the trail continued mostly flat throughout the morning. Like many recent days, we passed several bodies of water. We weren't really sure how one would get to Wadleigh Pond Rd., a gravel path just before Crescent Pond. Since this was one of the Wilderness roads we had chosen not to use, Molar Man had not figured out how to arrive here from Jo-Mary.

When we did reach "our" Wilderness road, Sweet Tooth was visiting with two others. Molar Man and I had crossed paths with them, Double Nickel and Rich, yesterday. Rich, a section-hiker from Georgia who had begun his quest of completing the Appalachian Trail over three decades earlier, couldn't believe his good fortune of finding trail magic in such a remote area. We all laughed as Birdman, another surprised hiker, walked up.

Each of these hikers, who were following a traditional approach to the 100 Mile Wilderness, showed interest in the Don's Brother Method.

"I had no idea you could slackpack in here," Double Nickel noted. "Who would have ever thought I'd be having a cold soda by a Volvo on this stretch of trail."

Nor did I contemplate being able to shuttle and slackpack this remote area of Maine when I first became interested in the A.T. over a decade ago. But we live and learn. As I sat on the ground and leaned against a tire of the car,

The Don's Brother Method

I reflected on my hike. I had hiked 2151.9 miles and 161 days but only spent 19 nights in the woods. I doubted that it was a record; however, I marveled at how my task had been accomplished.

"I think you may just have something with this Don's Brother Method," Rich noted. "There are probably lots of hikers who would prefer a bed and a hot meal every day over shelters and trail food."

Looking down at his filthy pants and muddy boots, a rather "ripe" Birdman chuckled in agreement. "I'll take the hot shower and steak right now," he added.

None accepted our offer of a ride into Millinocket. Instead, they preferred to spend two or three more nights in the woods before summit day. I understood. I admit there was a small part of me that wanted the full wilderness experience as well. Then on second thought, I remembered the room at the Katahdin Inn. There would be no more trail nights for me. Still, I respected my fellow sojourners who chose every night in the woods, and I understood their choice.

Bidding the three goodbye, Molar Man, Sweet Tooth, and I found our way back to Jo-Mary Rd. from Pollywog Stream, and from there back to ME 11. Since it was early afternoon, we again drove to Baxter State Park for more investigation. This time we made our way to the Katahdin Stream Campground where most thru-hikers spend their last night on the trail before summit day. No one was to be seen on the now warm, peaceful day.

We walked across a short bridge to another Ranger Station. Here we were given instructions for summiting. We signed in, indicating that our summit day would be September 2. A pile of daypacks lay in a corner of the small room. The ranger said that they were provided for those who didn't want to hike with all their gear to the top of Katahdin.

"We've rarely hiked with all of our gear for any part of this hike," I told the ranger without trying to be flippant. Listening to me give him a brief outline of the DBM, he smiled, shaking his head.

"There are all types, I suppose," he stated.

The ranger also offered some weather advice: "Be careful of potentially dangerous conditions, like rain and heavy wind. The slippery rocks could be disastrous. But then, few would ever climb Katahdin if they waited for a perfect day."

From Baxter we next headed back up Golden Rd. for Millinocket. After a quick stop at the motel, the three of us ventured downtown to the Appalachian Trail Café. A favorite among thru-hikers, most frequent the establishment after completing the trail. Our trio decided a late lunch was in order even though we were still three days out.

Colorful tiles adorned the café's ceiling. Each year celebratory thru-hikers pen their trail names on one of the tiles, often along with tiny pictures and designs, after successfully making it from Springer to Katahdin. I took a few minutes to peruse the signatures while waiting for my sandwich.

Looking mainly at the class of 2013, I located the names of several hikers that I met along my journey. There were a few I hadn't seen since Georgia; others I had met for the first time only a couple of weeks earlier. It was good to know that each had made it and had signed a ceiling tile as confirmation of their accomplishment. It also felt satisfying anticipating a return to the café in three days to add my name to the list.

After a long lunch and a stroll up the two block, main business district of Penobscot Ave., we drove back to the inn. I lingered for a while in the lobby, hoping perhaps to see other thru-hikers who had already completed their treks. Having seen Barking Spider and Stretch earlier in the day, I knew that they, along with a few others, were enjoying a night at the motel before beginning their homeward travel.

Once again, the morning of day 162 commenced at 5:00. After two days of motel, do-it-yourself breakfasts, I needed a change. So I hurriedly hustled over to McDonald's for Hotcakes and Sausage while Molar Man consumed another of the spongy waffles. He and Sweet Tooth were loading up the Volvo when I returned.

Today would be the last in the Wilderness. It would also be the last that we would have to pay the $12 entrance at Jo-Mary Rd. At this point in my hike I really wasn't thinking much about money. Any budget that I may have considered when planning the hike had gone out the window over five months earlier in Georgia. As I forked over the cash this morning, my mind was on

The Don's Brother Method

the 17.2 miles left to hike to Abol Bridge. *The A.T. Guide* showed a seemingly flat line of trail with only five potential water crossings.

Like clockwork, Molar Man and I took our first steps on the trail at exactly 7:00. My buddy has the plan down to a science. For almost ten miles the trail remained about as level as I've ever seen it. We cruised all morning. Other than a brief stop at the Rainbow Stream Lean-to, we kept moving. After a short ascent up Rainbow Ledges, we took a break at the Hurd Brook Lean-to for lunch. From there we easily arrived at Golden Rd. before 2:30, marking the end of the 100 Mile Wilderness.

Even though I had hiked this stretch using my Don's Brother Method, I took a moment to pause and think about those who had been in the Wilderness for six to eight days. They must be enormously relieved to be back in civilization. The campground store, which sells burgers and sandwiches, must be a welcome sight. I'm sure many a hungry hiker has stopped in before moving on up the trail.

Sweet Tooth was waiting at the bridge to take our picture. Even though the car was there, we decided to walk another 0.4 miles up the road to where the trail moves back into the woods for today's ending point. We would return here tomorrow to cover the final 10.0 mile section leading up to summit day.

Today would be one of our shortest commutes since Monson. The distance from Golden Rd. back to Millinocket is a mere 19 miles. In any other part of the trail, this shuttle would seem extreme. In Maine it was commonplace. I just felt fortunate to be in the company of the couple from Ohio. I had spent a considerable amount of money since leaving Georgia, but I would have spent a lot more if I had been using paid shuttles for the Wilderness.

Molar Man and I had taken seven days to cover the 100 miles. We had only spent one night in the woods and slackpacked five of the days. Sweet Tooth had been able to access seldom-used, or no-longer-used, logging roads to drop us off and pick us up each day. We had entered and/or exited the Wilderness via the Katahdin Ironworks Rd. twice, and by Jo-Mary Rd. the other three days. There were navigational challenges; however, we successfully found all the places where the A.T. crosses a road, no matter how remote.

I would not advise attempting to use the Don's Brother Method in the 100 Mile Wilderness without a good deal of planning. Molar Man and Sweet Tooth had all of the forest road maps, a good GPS system, and scouted out the areas in advance of the day's hike. Without their assistance, I would not have been able to move through this section with my plan.

As I have stated earlier, there are sources that will provide shuttles to and from the Wilderness in Monson and in Millinocket. Phil at Appalachian Trail Adventures in Monson and Ole Man at the Appalachian Lodge in Millinocket are great resources. But like 5:30 had told me back in Erwin, it's expensive.

So after the short 19 mile drive back to the Katahdin Inn, I spent the remainder of the afternoon relaxing. Later in the evening Molar Man, Sweet Tooth, and I joined Susquehanna Slim and his wife, Jodie, for a celebratory meal in town. Slim had summited the previous day. With an obvious anxious feeling, I quizzed my old hiking buddy throughout the appetizers and main course. Slim did his best to alleviate any fears I might have. And as day 162 came to a happy end, in many ways he did ease my mind.

Since Molar Man and I only had a 10.0 mile day planned on the morning of day 163, my good friend agreed that we could delay our wake-up call by an hour. I duplicated yesterday's breakfast with a trip to McDonald's. Shortly thereafter, we were on our way back to Golden Rd. Thinking about Slim's advice, I reminded myself that I still had the short section to complete today before focusing on Katahdin.

At 7:30 Molar Man and I stepped back on the A.T. off of Golden Rd. For about a mile the trail followed a dirt road before turning into the woods. Just as *The A.T. Guide* had indicated, most of today's hike was quite comfortable. Other than having to circumvent a rather swollen Nesowadnehunk Stream, no other obstacles presented themselves. A few roots, some rocks, and a little mud were mere minor hindrances.

We took a side trail to view Big Niagara Falls and another to enjoy briefly Little Niagara Falls. Molar Man and I both wondered how the two had gotten their names. All continued pleasant. I even found myself feeling relaxed for much of the short hiking day.

The Don's Brother Method

Upon reaching the Katahdin Stream Campground, we again visited the Ranger Station to officially register to climb Katahdin the following morning. Since we had talked with another ranger two days previously, neither of us had any questions of the helpful young man. When he mentioned the daypacks stacked in a corner, this time I just responded with a smile and a "no thank you." Details didn't seem necessary.

From the park it was back to Millinocket and one final night at the Katahdin Inn. It seemed appropriate to visit McDonald's one final time as well. I also made a last run to the Subway across ME 11 to buy lunch for the hike up Katahdin. Having dined on the Subway Melt on several mountains, I thought it appropriate to make that six inch sub my final A.T. meal. It felt good to be able to be thinking about so many "finals."

Arriving back in the lobby of the motel, I noticed a few familiar faces. To my delight, I was able to chat with Goose and All the Way as well as Torch. Each had been a significant part of my hike. Remembering where our paths had first crossed, I thought about just how important the trail community is. Although there was a very good chance that I would never see any of them after this moment, for a few weeks they had been family. For the remainder of the evening of day 163, I tried to stay calm.

Reflecting on what had happened in my life over the past five months and ten days, I above all was grateful. I was grateful to Molar Man and Sweet Tooth for allowing me to share their Volvo. I was grateful to Banzai's brother, Mike, who had spent two weeks providing support in Vermont and New Hampshire. I was grateful for all the many others who had shuttled me, often from remote stretches of trail, to a town and a bed. I was grateful for all of those who had helped make the Don's Brother Method a success. As I prepared to sleep this final night before summit day, I offered up a prayer of thanksgiving. With one final climb remaining, I still couldn't believe that I had hiked 2,180.8 miles on the Appalachian Trail.

On the morning of day 164 I awoke filled with apprehension. With rain forecast by early afternoon, Molar Man suggested that we plan to arrive at Baxter State Park when the gates opened at 6:00. With ominous looking gray skies overhead, we both seemed edgy on the drive from Millinocket. Sweet

Tooth attempted to lift the gloom in the Volvo to no avail. Molar Man and I were both tense.

At the main gate to the park we only had to wait a few minutes before we were allowed entrance. My anxiety grew as we travelled the gravelly road back to the campground. I prayed that the rain would hold off until the predicted 2:00 PM shower. For a brief moment a slither of blue sky appeared, only to disappear almost as rapidly as it had occurred. When we signed the trailhead register at 6:30, our hope was to be signing it again in seven hours or less.

From the campground, the initial segment of trail allowed my hiking buddy and me to maintain a fairly quick pace. After about one mile, however, the climbing began. First it was reminiscent of the Whites with slanted rocks, yet also with some small trees to hold onto for balance. Unfortunately, this terrain was short-lived.

Within another mile we found ourselves above tree line, confronted with what would be two miles of precipitous rock scrambling. And just as we approached the most challenging portion of rocks, the rain began. At first, it was a mere sprinkle. Then the wind strengthened and the light rain became a steady moderate drizzle.

For 163 days of thru-hiking the Appalachian Trail what I had feared most was wet rocks. In fact, I postponed a section in New Hampshire and took a day off in Maine to avoid the slippery menaces. Now here I was, about two-thirds up Katahdin, in a downpour with 60 mile per hour winds. One of my water bottles fell from my pack and toppled down the mountain. There was no turning back. Molar Man and I just had to persevere and keep moving. That's exactly what we did.

From the Tableland we ascended again. We reached Thoreau Spring as the wind speed again increased. It was difficult to stand. The rain subsided briefly as the famous sign marking the end of the A.T. came into sight. With the weather continuing to deteriorate, Molar Man and I did not linger. I had envisioned remaining on the summit for half an hour, taking pictures and enjoying the view. On this inclement day, however, my thoughts turned to survival. After only a few quick pictures, we began the descent. It was 10:00.

Going down proved to be as harrowing an experience as the ascent had been. In fact, it required more caution, especially as the gusting wind continued. I was literally blown over twice. The other of my water bottles blew from its pack pocket to disappear over the edge of a large boulder. Molar Man and I both shivered in totally soaked clothing. Hypothermia crossed my mind. I had not felt this cold since Tennessee.

Gingerly making my way down the extremely wet rocks, I remained patient. Often having to drop from one large slab onto another, I concentrated on a balanced landing. I also began to think that if either of us got injured, there would probably be no chance of a rescue in these conditions. Looking back, Molar Man and I were both exceedingly fortunate to make it back below tree line without a mishap.

When we finally reached the trailhead where we had registered our hike seven and one-half hours earlier, I think we were both grateful to have reached the summit of Katahdin as well as relieved to be alive. My only disappointment was that we had completed the hike more quickly than I had anticipated. As a result my family had not arrived at the campground to see me come off of the trail for one last time.

Thankfully, Sweet Tooth turned the heater inside the Volvo to its maximum setting while Molar Man and I rapidly shed our wet clothes for dry layers. Still, my teeth chattered. They both offered to wait for Linda, Lisa, Brent, and Lori to show up. I thought it better that we just start driving toward the park entrance in expectation of meeting them on the way. We did. I didn't know whether to smile or cry when I spotted my wife, sister-in-law, nephew and his wife, pull along beside us in their rental van. Still shaking, I chose to stay in the warm car for the return ride to Millinocket. The van followed.

Back at the Katahdin Inn smiles abounded. After a hot shower I sat on a stuffed chair in the lobby of the motel and unloaded my pack. A now soggy Subway Melt lay in its plastic wrapper on top of my equally wet spare shirt. Despite a rain cover, everything in the pack was wet. It didn't really matter. I was dry and safe. I had hiked 2,185.9 miles from Springer Mountain in Georgia to the summit of Mount Katahdin, Baxter Peak, and the northern terminus of the Appalachian Trail. I felt both relieved and happy.

For the past two weeks I had been promising Molar Man and Sweet Tooth a lobster dinner after we summited. At the A.T. Café in Millinocket, however, lobster was not on the menu. Steak dinners would have to suffice. The couple from Ohio, who had been my greatest support for well over 500 miles of my hike, were happy to join my family and me for a celebratory meal. Sitting in the small restaurant among friends and those I loved, I think my greatest feeling was simply relief.

After the late lunch I said my goodbyes to the two people I had been around daily for the past month. For Molar Man, it was back to complete a short section in New Hampshire and then the part of the trail he had omitted in New York. For me, it was a ride in the back of a van, sitting beside my wife, to Bangor, where another room awaited. It would be the last and the best bed of all those I had had the good fortune to occupy on my journey from Georgia to Maine.

The duration of my thru-hike of the Appalachian Trail was 164 days, beginning on March 23 and ending on September 2, 2013. The final night after my summit of Katahdin, would be exactly the 100th that I would spend in a motel. There had been 24 nights in hostels and 16 in shelters. I had gone to bed in a B & B on nine nights, private homes five, in an AMC hut four times, and only tented on three occasions. I had also spent two nights in a cabin and one in a condo. I had indeed thru-hiked the Appalachian Trail and rarely slept in the woods.

CHAPTER 17

Another Bed in Bangor

Of all the hikers I have met, Don's Brother is the king of planning ahead and executing that plan to a 'T.' His timing of arriving at and departing from the trail and towns, and keeping up the calories, on and off the trail, are not easy things to do. His method is a good thing to think about and learn from, especially for some of us older folks.

STEVE LaBOMBARD (BENNINGTON, VT)

HAVING MY FAMILY ARRIVE IN Maine to share the completion of my thru-hike of the Appalachian Trail was truly special. I would probably never have undertaken the journey had it not been for the illness and death of my younger brother, Don. Lisa, Don's widow, had been with me when I set out from Springer and had promised to be at Baxter on summit day. Accompanied by her and Don's son and my nephew, Brent, his wife, Lori, and Linda, she kept that promise. Each seemed as genuinely proud and excited over my accomplishment as I was.

In Bangor, thanks to Lisa, I finally upgraded. The Hilton Garden Inn far surpassed any of the humble abodes where I had laid my head over the past five months, eleven days. Luxury even came to mind. After leisurely unpacking, Linda and I joined the others for a late meal in the motel's dining room. Then Lisa drove to the Bangor airport to pick up Rachel, who had flown in from New York.

Not having seen my daughter since I took the train from Port Jervis to have lunch with her in the City, I almost cried when I opened the motel room door to her beaming smile. Knowing we had tomorrow to spend together, I was just happy to get a hug. It had been an emotional day. I had been awake almost twenty hours when I finally lay my head on the softest of pillows, to enjoy one of the most satisfying nights of sleep in my life.

The following morning we enjoyed a scrumptious breakfast buffet before embarking on a drive to Bar Harbor. It felt so good to be able to walk all day without constantly looking downward. Finally, I could stroll along a sandy beach without having to fear a fall. The rocky shore line of the picturesque New England town did bring back a few memories from days on the A.T. But now I could savor the beauty, knowing the rigors of trail life were in my past.

Even though I had experienced many meals in restaurants over the past five months of hiking, none compared to the two seafood feasts I consumed on day 165. First came lunch overlooking the bay in Bar Harbor. Then back in Bangor I selected an equally appetizing entre for my evening meal.

Later in our motel room I asked Linda, "Do you remember me telling you that I was going to find as many beds and restaurants as I could during my thru-hike?"

"Yes," she responded. "And it looks like you kept your promise. So, how many were there?"

"I haven't added them all up yet, but I think I only spent 19 nights in the woods. All the rest were in motels, B & B's, hostels, cabins, and a few other places with beds."

Just as I had smiled six months earlier at our kitchen table, I smiled again. I had walked 2,185.9 miles from Springer Mountain in Georgia to Maine's Mount Katahdin over 164 days. I had hiked every step north, always following the white blazes, and I had not gone home over the course of the journey. All my goals had been met. Tomorrow I would fly back to Georgia a happy man. I had honored my brother's memory and become a part of a small community of those who had successfully thru-hiked the Appalachian Trail.

CHAPTER 18

A Hike Without a Tent

Not only is Don's story captivating but so is your method of hiking the trail. Now others are taking up your hiking style and joining you. You should write a book.

BOB "STEADY ON" SCHILLO (SEWICKLEY, PA)

OVER THE FINAL MONTH OF my hike I adopted a mantra of sorts. When difficulties arose, I reminded myself that "Every step I took was a step that I would never have to take again." At least not unless I wanted to take it again. After over five months on the Appalachian Trail, all I really wanted to do was be finished and go home. That was in New Hampshire. Arguably the most challenging state, Maine, still remained to be tackled.

Every day of the 164 presented a mental challenge. Some days the trail offered more than others. Somehow, however, I persevered and attained the goal I had set out to accomplish. From the early days, I had a plan. For me, that plan revolved around towns. There was never a doubt in my mind that I could walk from Georgia to Maine. There was always a doubt from the first night on the trail on Hawk Mountain as to whether I could survive in the woods.

I don't mean necessarily survive from the standpoint of staying alive. I never feared for my safety. I just never felt comfortable performing the daily tasks that most hikers view as routine. For instance, pitching a tent has always been somewhat difficult for me. The main reason I began the hike with a ten year-old, less than trail-worthy one was because I couldn't find a suitable replacement with which I was comfortable.

After only three nights in the faulty structure, I simply decided to forgo a shelter altogether. That was possibly not a wise decision. Had I encountered any situations where I needed protection from the elements, for instance had I gotten injured, I could have found myself in a very dangerous position. Thankfully, that never occurred. Still, if I were going to attempt another thru-hike of the A.T., I would consider carrying a light tent or tarp, at least on days that I did not have pre-arranged support waiting for me at the end of a day.

Other than the tent, I wouldn't make many changes with gear. I didn't carry a stove until Hiawassee. From there I had one in my pack, but never used it. When I reached Newfound Gap I sent it home. Since I only stayed in the woods 19 nights, I really didn't miss the hot meals.

If I were hiking again, I still wouldn't tote one. By Virginia I met many other thru-hikers who had discarded their stoves for various reasons. Sure, hot food beats cold any time; however, there are some downsides to travelling with a kitchen as well. Fuel has to be located and carried, which adds weight. The cooking hiker also needs a pot, something to clean it with, and something to carry all these items in, which also increases the weight of one's pack.

Since I didn't carry a tent or stove, and since my pack rarely contained more than one day's food supply, my pack weight stayed low. The farther one gets up the trail, the less one really finds absolutely necessary. Believe me, a lighter pack obviously makes for a more enjoyable hike. Some gear is essential. Some items are not. Each hiker has to decide for himself what he needs to ensure success of a thru-hike of the A.T. So many factors may contribute to failure. An excessively heavy pack, due to unnecessary gear, should not be one of them.

CHAPTER 19

Fine-Tuning the DBM

Slackpacking was pretty common coming into and leaving trail towns like Hot Springs and Damascus. I met a few people, like Molar Man, who were attempting to slackpack the entire trail with a dedicated support person (Sweet Tooth). Don's Brother was the only person I heard of who hiked the whole trail with a support team that was often made up on the fly. It's amazing that he pulled it off. It took a lot of work to constantly get to and from the trail on an almost daily basis. It gave him access to a large number of 'trail people' as well as 'town people.' His method also gave him more opportunities to talk about his brother, which I know was an important part of his hike.

WALT "SUSQUEHANNA SLIM" KRZASTEK (BETHLEHEM, PA)

OTHER THAN A MINOR GEAR addition, what other changes would I make, if I were attempting to thru-hike the Appalachian Trail again? There were several hostels where I missed staying for one reason or another. If I were thru-hiking the A.T. again, I think I might forgo a motel occasionally for a hostel. On the other hand, there were a few hostels that I would avoid on the second trip as well.

To begin with I would try to eliminate most of the 19 nights I spent in the woods. In some instances this task looks easy; in others, it might be impossible. State by state, these are places where I now see that my hike could have been altered. After all, I know a little bit more about roads along the A.T. than I did on March 23, 2013 at Springer.

Georgia: The first state at the Southern terminus of the Appalachian Trail is among the easiest to slackpack. The first change I would make would be on day one. Rather than stopping at the Hawk Mountain shelter area to tent, I would have hiked an additional 0.5 miles to Hightower Gap, where USFS Rd. 42 crosses. From there I would have arranged a shuttle to the Hiker Hostel near Suches, GA. I could have stayed two nights at the hostel, walked with a light pack the first day on the trail, and have eliminated one of the 19 nights in the woods immediately.

The second change that I would make in GA would be between Unicoi Gap and Dicks Creek Gap. I could have easily continued on from Addis Gap, where I tented on day six, to US 76 that leads to Hiawassee. For me, this would be a very doable 16.7 miles, even with a full pack. Or, I could have pre-arranged to have my gear shuttled ahead from Helen to Hiawassee. The Blueberry Patch, where I stayed in 2013, is now closed. The Top of Georgia hostel, however, offers shuttles and will assist with slackpacking.

I could have begun my thru-hike of the A.T. without spending any nights in the woods in the 78.5 miles of my home state.

North Carolina/Tennessee: My third night in the woods, and my last to use a tent, occurred at Deep Gap, NC. Even though it is a long shuttle, I would leave the trail here via USFS Rd. 71 for Franklin. After setting up a base camp at a motel, I would return to the trail at Deep Gap the following day and hike to Mooney Gap, USFS Rd. 83/Ball Creek Rd. to again shuttle to Franklin. The next day I would continue from Mooney Gap to Winding Stair Gap, and again spend the night in Franklin.

I would have erased two more nights in the woods, still having hiked the 24.4 miles between Deep Gap and Winding Stair Gap in two days. Because these are reasonably lengthy distances to town, it would certainly help to have your own support here rather than having to pay a shuttle provider. After Franklin, I don't see any reasons to make changes until after the Smokies.

The one section of trail where it is seemingly impossible to get off the trail, with the exception of Newfound Gap, is the Great Smoky Mountains National

Park. There are just no roads. Other than a few horse trails, I couldn't see any viable access between Fontana Dam and Clingman's Dome. Being so close to US 441 at Newfound Gap, I wouldn't utilize the Clingman's Dome Rd. exit.

There are some usable trails off the A.T. between US 441 and Davenport Gap; however, I'm not sure it would be worth the trouble to shuttle out and back into the park. If I were going to attempt another thru-hike, I would probably still spend three nights in shelters in the Smokies. After my last night in the Smokies at Tri-Corner Knob shelter, I didn't spend another night in the woods for 328 trail miles.

At times, I would make some changes with daily mileage and shuttles. Because I had a friend to pick me up at Davenport Gap and also at Lemon Gap, I was able to stay over 30 miles from the trail at Lake Junaluska. There are closer towns, but again, shuttles from either of these Gaps, or nearby Max Patch, can be expensive. Having a support person here, rather than having to employ a paid shuttler, would certainly help.

One of the most expensive shuttles I paid for was from Devil Fork Gap, NC 212, at trail mile 309, to Erwin. If I had not pre-arranged a ride with someone from the Hemlock Hollow hostel, I possibly could have hitched to town from here. If not, Tom "10K" Bradford, from Erwin, would have been a better shuttle option.

Virginia/West Virginia: The first night I spent in the woods in Virginia, and also the first in the woods since the Smokies, could have been eliminated. The 23.0 miles between VA 683 near Atkins to the Chestnut Knob shelter were grueling. In hindsight, I should have stayed an additional night at the motel in Marion after slackpacking the 11.8 from VA 683/US 11 to VA 42. A conveniently located parking area sits just off the trail here.

Upon returning to the trail at VA 42, I would cover 17.2 to VA 623 and shuttle into Bland. This would add a day to my hike, taking the place of the day I had already eliminated in Georgia. The following day I could leave my gear at the motel in Bland and slackpack the 15.7 miles from VA 623 back to Bland. Rather than two nights in Marion, one in a shelter, and two in Bland, I would tweak the DBM to include three nights at a motel in each of the trail towns. Paid shuttles can be arranged from both.

The next two nights I spent in the woods of Virginia could be avoided. Since I was coming off of an Achilles injury after leaving Daleville, I didn't want to try to cover too many miles in a day for a while. Healthy, however, I would combine the three days from Jennings Creek, VA 614 to US 501 into two days totaling only 28.5 miles. The Blue Ridge Parkway crosses the trail several times between this stretch, and a ride into Glasgow or even Buena Vista can be arranged.

The next night on the trail, at Pinefield Hut in the Shenandoah National Park, could have been averted. The A.T. intersects Skyline Parkway numerous times throughout the park. On another hike I would pre-arrange a ride from the drive into Elkton and spend two nights in a motel there rather than one. I also would possibly skip Skyland Resort because of the expense, opting instead to shuttle or hitch on the Drive into Luray. I would also consider shuttling from Luray a second night before getting to US 522 and Front Royal.

As I arrived at the Appalachian Trail Conservancy in Harper's Ferry, West Virginia, the mental half-way point of the A.T., and after 74 days on the trail, I had only spent eleven of those nights in the woods. Eight of those eleven could have easily been eliminated.

Maryland: I spent no nights in the woods in the second shortest state on the A.T.

Pennsylvania: The Keystone state is by far one of the easiest to slackpack. Roads abound. For many miles the trail parallels I-81 and passes close to a number of fairly large towns. Motels and restaurants can be found in close proximity to the trail almost daily.

The only night I spent on the trail in PA was at the Allentown Hiking Club Shelter after a 22.2 mile day with a full pack. On a second trip up the A.T. I would entertain various options between Port Clinton and Palmerton. I hiked this stretch in two days; however, I might increase it to three. I would consider walking a short day to Reservoir Rd. and then shuttling back for another night in Hamburg. The following day I would continue to PA 309, Blue Mountain Summit Rd., where there is a small motel only a few yards from the trail. From there I would move on to Palmerton the next day.

Another option here would be to divide the 39.5 mile section into three days by using a shuttle from a parking lot 13.9 trail miles north of Port Clinton. From there on the following day, the hike could end at Bake Oven Knob Rd., a distance of 17.6 miles, leaving only 8.9 miles to Palmerton. With this plan, I probably would pass Palmerton as an overnight stay and move on to Little Gap Rd., near Danielsville, where there is a B & B. From this road a shuttle into East Stroudsburg could also be arranged. Again, there are just a lot of opportunities to use roads in Pennsylvania.

New Jersey: Like PA, I spent one night on the trail in New Jersey at the Gren Anderson Shelter. On another hike I would probably stop at US 206, Culvers Gap, near Branchville, stay in a motel, and then hike from there on to US 23 near Port Jervis the following day. As in Pennsylvania, there are several roads that the A.T. crosses in New Jersey. Shuttles can be arranged to a number of nearby towns for a night in a motel in this area.

New York: The only night I stayed on the trail in New York was at the RPH Shelter on Hortontown Rd. Since pizza is regularly delivered to this shelter, a shuttle can be arranged to a motel in Poughquag or to the Duches Motor Inn near Wingdale, where I spent one night. On a second hike, I think I would stay at this motel for two nights and slackpack from Hortontown Rd. to NY 55, or possibly on to County Rd. 20, West Dover Rd., near Pawling. It was from NY 55 that I had no difficulty hitching to the Duches Inn.

Connecticut, Massachusetts, and Vermont: I spent no nights in the woods in any of these states. In fact, after the RPH shelter, I didn't sleep in the woods again for 474.8 trail miles, with the exception of four of the AMC Huts in the Whites. As I've stated before, the huts were more hostel-like, especially when I paid for a bunk.

New Hampshire: Ironically, the last night on the trail in New Hampshire at the Gentian Pond Shelter could have been avoided. On another hike I would utilize the Austin Brook Trail to Mill Brook Rd. rather than staying in the woods. From the road a shuttle can be arranged to the Cabin near Andover. My hiking buddies and I used this plan the morning after the night at the shelter, due to weather. That side-trail hike could have been accomplished the previous afternoon just as easily.

Maine: Looking back on my nights in the woods through the first thirteen of the fourteen states that comprise the Appalachian Trail, I have determined that I could eliminate all of them, except the three nights in the Smokies, with relative ease. Maine, however, poses more challenges. I stayed in four shelters during the 283 miles of the Pine Tree State. Considering the remoteness and isolation of the area, pre-planning is essential.

Even though there are some roads and spur trails leading to the Appalachian Trail between the Gentian Pond Shelter and Grafton Notch, these sometimes unmarked logging roads are not always navigable. Furthermore, the side trails can be just as formidable and time-consuming as the A.T. With this said, I imagine I would still stay in the woods at the Full Goose Shelter the day before tackling the Mahoosuc Notch. Considered by many to be the most difficult mile on the entire trail, an equally hard segment, including the Mahoosuc Arm and Old Speck Mountain, follows.

The second shelter I used in Maine was Poplar Ridge. There is a Woods road 2.8 miles past the lean-to; however, Molar Man and I couldn't figure out how to use it. With help from someone with knowledge of the area, that road could be an option for leaving the trail for a second night in Rangeley.

Our next night in the woods came at the Moxie Bald Mountain Lean-to after a 13.6 mile hike from Pleasant Pond Rd. On another thru-hike attempt I think that I would continue on an additional 8.8 miles to a paved Shirley-Blanchard Rd. from where I would head to Greenville. With a slackpack and plenty of daylight, this is a manageable day. There are other gravel roads between Moxie Bald and Shirley-Blanchard, but they may not be passable.

My final night in the woods occurred at the Logan Brook Lean-to in the 100 Mile Wilderness. There is a woods road just past the shelter at B Inlet Brook, but Molar Man and I couldn't find access to it on our scouting expedition. The gravel Kodadjo-B Rd. from Jo-Mary Rd. is usable; however, a 21 mile day would be necessary to reach it from the A.T. crossing at the West Branch of the Pleasant River. Exiting the Wilderness from one of these spots could be accomplished.

So, if I were going to attempt another thru-hike of the Appalachian Trail, I would probably only plan six nights in the woods: three in the Smokies and the other three in Maine. Even though two of the three in Maine could probably be avoided, the seldom-used woods roads might not be good options. But, it could be done. There are those in the area who know the trail much better than I do who could assist with the planning.

Again, I'm only speculating on changes that I would make. With good support, advanced planning, and utilization of various side trails, I believe a thru-hike of the Appalachian Trail can be accomplished without spending any nights in the woods. This type of hike would obviously be more expensive and require precise coordination between the hiker and his support person or paid shuttle drivers. The Don's Brother Method is not for everyone, but again, it is an option.

CHAPTER 20

Hike Your Own Hike

Before hiking the AT, my opinion of the Don's Brother Method would have been negative. In a way I felt that people who hiked in this fashion were cheapening the experience and in some way robbing us all. However, after hiking the AT, I find that my thoughts on this particular method have changed—perhaps 180 degrees. The way one chooses to sleep is an individual choice. What's the difference between a hostel or hotel and a tent or a shelter, except the obvious warmth/coolness, a shower and proper bathroom facilities? Staying out of hotels and hostels was best for me. Who's to say what is best for the individual other than himself? Every hiker just needs to make sure he/she hikes the entire trail if he/she wants to claim the achievement.

KIRK "OB" EATON (COVINGTON, GA)

ONE OF THE MOST OFTEN-VOICED slogans heard along the Appalachian Trail is "Hike your own hike." Simply, it means that every person who arrives on Springer Mountain with the expectation of reaching the summit of Mount Katahdin should hike in a manner that best suits him. Whether we are talking about the number of miles hiked each day, the weight of one's pack, the choices of gear, or a plethora of other factors, each individual has to make his own decisions, regardless of what others may suggest.

The Don's Brother Method

A trap into which many would-be thru-hikers fall early in their journey is following what others are doing. Some hike too many miles before their bodies have acclimated themselves to the trail. Others let hiking companions dictate where they camp or if and when they go into town. A few compromise the integrity of their hikes (like blue or yellow blazing) because they see someone else making this choice. Many just find it too stressful or challenging to plan for themselves.

Unfortunately a good number of those who fall into any of the above categories are not successful. Only about twenty-five percent or fewer of those who plan to hike the entire trail make it. The remainder quit somewhere along the way for a variety of reasons. Some get injured, often due to pushing themselves beyond what they are capable of early in the hike. Some get homesick, missing family and friends. Many run out of money. A few have emergencies that force them to abandon their hikes. Sadly, a large number of those who quit do so because they did not "hike their own hikes."

As I stated at the beginning of this book, having hiked over 1000 miles of the Appalachian Trail in sections over nine years, I had a really good understanding of just about every aspect of the trail. I also had a really good understanding of who I was as a hiker, and more importantly, as an outdoorsman. I enjoyed hiking enormously, but I really didn't like much about the camping component of a thru-hike.

Before I even left my home in Columbus, I already had decided that I would begin the hike in the traditional way. But I had also promised myself that I would alter my plan to hike more unconventionally as soon as I grew weary of the conventional manner. That happened much more quickly than I anticipated. After a wet tent on the first night, a calorie-depleted second day's walk, and snow and ice on day three, the Don's Brother Method was put into action.

It didn't take long for me to determine that the only way I was going to get to Maine was by utilizing a lot of towns. My first base was in Helen, Georgia, the alpine-themed tourist town that many thru-hikers skip. The Best Western on US 75, however, was just what I needed. I was able to stay in the same room two nights, slackpack one day, feast on a breakfast buffet in front of a roaring fire two mornings, and consume three meals at Wendy's. After those first three challenging days, Helen invigorated me.

Between Unicoi Gap (where the A.T. crosses the highway leading to Helen) and Franklin, North Carolina, I tried again to hike more traditionally. I tented two more nights and spent one in a shelter. But by the time I checked out of the Microtel on the morning of my eleventh day on the trail, I wouldn't sleep on the trail again until the Smokies. After those three nights, it would be over 300 trail miles before I would find myself spending a night in the woods.

So with over 2000 miles still to be traveled, I had decided that "hiking my own hike" meant finding all the beds and restaurants that were remotely close to the Appalachian Trail. With spending only 19 nights in the woods during a 164 day trek, I think I did a pretty good job of following my plan.

There were many factors that contributed to my success. Mainly, I seemed to encounter the right people at just the right time. Molar Man and Sweet Tooth proved to be life-savers on more than one occasion. Having their support for almost a quarter of my hike made a huge difference.

Hooking up with Pilgrim and Banzai in Massachusetts, and later with Susquehanna Slim in Vermont, enabled me to employ my method more easily. Mike, Banzai's brother, also provided essential aid when he shuttled the group for two weeks. All of these friends were key components to my being able to "hike my own hike." They bought in to the Don's Brother Method, and we each benefited from the camaraderie we established.

I think the best advice that I could give to someone contemplating a thru-hike of the Appalachian Trail is simply to "hike your own hike." Make a plan, but be willing to change it. Purchase good gear, but realize that gear itself doesn't guarantee success. Set yourself a budget, but be prepared to spend more money than you think you will spend. Familiarize yourself with the A.T., and if possible, do at least one short section hike prior to beginning a thru. Start alone, and do exactly what you want to do. You'll meet others along the way.

Above all, have a plan for when you feel like quitting. For me, it was to go to town. I realize that everyone doesn't have unlimited financial means, (nor did I), but the more you can spend, the better chance you will have for success. A restaurant meal, a hot shower, and a comfortable bed can do wonders for the body and the spirit. I'm extremely happy and proud that I accomplished my thru-hike of the Appalachian Trail. However, I'm not sure it would have occurred without the Don's Brother Method.

Appendix

Ending Locations and Accommodations

Day	Ending Location	Miles Hiked	Accommodations
1	Hawk Mountain	8.1	Tent
2	Woody Gap, GA 60	13.1	Hostel (Hiker Hostel)
3	Neels Gap, US 19	10.5	Cabin (Blood Mt. Cabins)
4	Hogpen Gap, GA 348	6.9	Motel (Best Western, Helen)
5	Unicoi Gap, GA 75	14.3*	Motel (Best Western, Helen)
6	Addis Gap	11.3	Tent
7	Dicks Creek Gap, US 76	5.4	Hostel (Blueberry Patch)
8	Deep Gap	15.8	Tent
9	Long Branch Shelter	17.1	Shelter
10	Winding Stair Gap, US 64	7.3	Motel (Microtel, Franklin)
11	Day Off	0.0	Motel (Microtel, Franklin)
12	Burningtown Gap	14.6	Hostel (Aquone)
13	NOC, US 19 & 74	12.9	Bunkhouse
14	Stecoah Gap, NC 143	13.4	Cabin in the Woods
15	Fontana Dam, NC 28	13.9*	Motel (Hike Inn)
16	Spence Field Shelter	17.9	Shelter
17	Double Springs Shelter	13.5	Shelter
18	Newfound Gap, US 441	10.8	Friend's Condo (Sevierville)
19	Tri-Corner Knob Shelter	15.6	Shelter
20	Davenport Gap, TN 32	15.7	Motel (Lake Junaluska)

21	Lemon Gap, NC 1182	21.4*	Motel (Lake Junaluska)
22	Hot Springs, NC	14.4	Elmer's Sunnybank Inn
23	Log Cabin Rd.	16.3	Hostel (Hemlock Hollow)
24	Devil Fork Gap, NC 212	18.7	Motel (Super 8, Erwin, TN)
25	Day Off	0.0	Motel (Super 8, Erwin)
26	Spivey Gap, US 19W	21.9*	Motel (Super 8, Erwin)
27	Nolichucky River, River Rd.	10.7*	Motel (Super 8, Erwin)
28	Iron Mountain Gap TN 107	20.6*	Motel (Super 8, Erwin)
29	Carvers Gap, TN 143	14.8*	Motel (Super 8, Erwin)
30	Buck Mountain Rd.	18.3*	Motel (Elizabethton, TN)
31	Dennis Cove Rd, USF 50	21.1*	Motel (Elizabethton, TN)
32	Wilbur Dam Rd.	13.0*	Appalachian Folk School
33	Low Gap, US 421	22.6*	Appalachian Folk School
34	Damascus, VA	15.2	Montgomery Homestead Inn
35	US 58	16.7*	Montgomery Homestead Inn
36	Massie Gap, US 58	14.0	Hostel (Troutdale Baptist)
37	Day Off	0.0	Hostel (Troutdale Baptist)
38	Dickey Gap, VA 650/16	18.3*	Hostel (Troutdale Baptist)
39	VA 16	14.6	Motel (Marion, VA)
40	VA 683	11.5*	Motel (Marion, VA)
41	Chestnut Knob Shelter	23.0	Shelter
42	US 52	21.7	Motel (Bland, VA)
43	VA 606	18.6*	Motel (Bland, VA)
44	Sugar Run Rd.	13.9	Hostel (Woods Hole)
45	Pearisburg, VA	10.4	Motel (Plaza, Pearisburg)

The Don's Brother Method

46	VA 635	21.7*	Motel (Plaza, Pearisburg)
47	Rocky Gap, VA 601	13.1*	Motel (Plaza, Pearisburg)
48	Craig Creek Rd., VA 621	16.8	Motel (HOJO, Daleville)
49	Newport Rd., VA 624	15.4*	Motel (HOJO)
50	Day Off	0.0	Motel (Super 8, Daleville)
51	Daleville, US 220	25.7*	Motel (Super 8)
52	Harvey's Knob, BRP 95.3	16.1*	Motel (Super 8)
53	Jennings Creek, VA 614	12.1	Motel (Super 8)
54	Injury	0.0	Motel (Super 8)
55	Injury	0.0	Motel (Super 8)
56	Injury	0.0	Motel (Comfort Inn)
57	Injury	0.0	Motel (Comfort Inn)
58	Bryant Ridge Shelter	3.8	Shelter
59	Thunder Hill Shelter	10.2	Shelter
60	US 501, VA 130	14.6	Motel (Buena Vista, VA)
61	BRP 51.7	10.8*	Motel (Buena Vista, VA)
62	US 60	11.0*	Motel (Buena Vista, VA)
63	Spy Rock Rd.	16.3	Dutch Haus B & B
64	Three Ridges Overlook	20.3*	Dutch Haus B & B
65	Rockfish Gap	18.8	Motel (Super 8, Waynesboro)
66	Black Rock Gap	19.1*	Motel (Super 8, Waynesboro)
67	Pinefield Hut	13.9	Shelter
68	Lewis Mt. Campground	19.9**	Motel (Elkton, VA)
69	Skyland	16.6	Motel (Skyland Resort)
70	Elkwallow Gap	18.3	Hostel (Front Royal)

71	US 522, Front Royal	19.1*	Hostel (Front Royal)
72	Ashby Gap, US 50/17	20.0*	Hostel (Bears Den)
73	Bears Den Rocks	13.5*	Hostel (Bears Den)
74	Harper's Ferry	19.8	Motel (Charlestown, WV)
75	Day Off	0.6*	Motel (Charlestown, WV)
76	Turners Gap, US Alt 40	17.5	Motel (Hagerstown, MD)
77	Day Off	0.0	Motel
78	Pen Mar Rd.	23.5*	Motel (Fayetteville, PA)
79	US 30	17.8*	Motel (Fayetteville, PA)
80	A.T. Museum, PA 233	19.5*	Motel (Carlisle, PA)
81	Boiling Springs, PA 174	19.6*	Motel (Carlisle, PA)
82	PA 850	16.5*	Motel (Off I-81)
83	PA 225	17.5*	Motel (Off I-81)
84	PA 443	25.6*	Motel (Off I-81)
85	PA 501	12.8*	Motel (Pine Grove, PA)
86	Day Off	0.0	Motel (Pine Grove, PA)
87	Port Clinton	24.1	Motel (Hamburg, PA)
88	Day Off	0.0	Motel (Hamburg, PA)
89	Allentown HC Shelter	22.2	Shelter
90	Palmerton, PA 873	17.3	Hostel
91	Wind Gap, PA 33	20.8*	Motel (East Stroudsburg, PA)
92	Delaware Water Gap	15.7	Motel (East Stroudsburg)
93	Blue Mtn Lakes Rd.	17.7*	Motel (East Stroudsburg)
94	Gren Anderson Shelter	13.6	Shelter
95	NJ 23	11.3	Motel (Port Jervis, NY)

96	Day Off (NYC)	0.0	Motel (Port Jervis, NY)
97	Vernon, NJ 94	20.6	Hostel (Episcopal Church)
98	Greenwood Lake, NY 17A	15.0	Motel (Greenwood Lk, NY)
99	NY 17	12.0	Motel (Ft. Montgomery, NY)
100	NY 9D	19.8*	Motel (Ft. Montgomery, NY)
101	US 9 & NY 403	5.8*	Motel (Ft. Montgomery, NY)
102	Hortontown Rd.	19.4	RPH Shelter
103	NY 55	12.3	Motel (Near Wingdale, NY)
104	Bulls Bridge Rd.	18.8	Cooper Creek B & B (Kent)
105	CT 4, Guinea Brook	18.3*	Cooper Creek B & B (Kent)
106	Falls Village, CT	14.0*	Maria McCabe's (Salisbury)
107	Undermountain Rd.	8.3*	Maria McCabe's
108	MA 41	17.8*	Maria McCabe's
109	MA 23	12.0	Motel (Great Barrington, MA)
110	Main Rd, Tyringham, MA	12.2*	Motel (Great Barrington, MA)
111	Washington Mt. Rd.	18.0*	Motel (Pittsfield, MA)
112	Main St., Cheshire, MA	18.3*	Motel (Williamstown, MA)
113	MA 2	14.7*	Motel (Williamstown, MA)
114	VT 9	18.4*	Motel (Bennington, VT)
115	Day Off	0.0	Motel (Bennington, VT)
116	USFS Rd. 71	20.6*	Motel (Bennington, VT)
117	VT 11 & 30	19.5*	Hostel (Manchester Center)
118	Danby-Landgrove Rd.	17.6*	Hostel (Manchester Center)
119	VT 103	14.8	Quality Inn (Rutland, VT)
120	US 4	18.4*	Quality Inn (Rutland, VT)

121	VT 12	22.3*	Quality Inn (Rutland, VT)
122	VT 14	13.0*	Super 8 (White River Junction)
123	Hanover, NH	9.9*	Super 8 (White River Junction)
124	Dorchester Rd.	17.5*	Super 8 (White River Junction)
125	NH 25A	16.0*	Rodeway Inn (Lincoln, NH)
126	NH 25	9.9*	Rodeway Inn (Lincoln, NH)
127	NH 112 (Kinsman Notch)	9.3*	Hostel (Lincoln, NH)
128	US 3 (Franconia Notch)	16.3*	Econo Lodge (Lincoln, NH)
129	Day Off	0.0	Econo Lodge (Lincoln, NH)
130	Galehead Hut	13.0	AMC Hut
131	US 302 (Crawford Notch)	14.7	Royalty Inn (Gorham, NH)
132	Lake of the Clouds Hut	11.2	AMC Hut
133	Mt. Washington	1.3	Royalty Inn (Gorham, NH)
134	Day Off (Gorham, NH)	0.0	Hiker's Paradise (Gorham)
135	Carter Notch Hut	6.2	AMC Hut
136	US 2	14.9	Hiker's Paradise (Gorham)
137	Madison Spring Hut	5.7	AMC Hut
138	NH 16 (Pinkham Notch)	7.8	Hiker's Paradise (Gorham)
139	Gentian Pond Shelter	11.8	Shelter
140	The Cabin	0.0	The Cabin (Andover, ME)
141	Full Goose Shelter	9.6	Shelter
142	ME 26 (Grafton Notch)	9.7	The Cabin (Andover, ME)
143	East B Hill Rd.	10.3*	The Cabin (Andover, ME)
144	South Arm Rd.	10.1*	The Cabin (Andover, ME)
145	ME 17	13.2*	The Cabin (Andover, ME)

The Don's Brother Method

146	ME 4	13.2*	Town & Lake Motel (Rangeley)
147	Poplar Ridge Lean-to	10.7	Shelter
148	Caribou Valley Rd.	13.2	Stratton Motel (Stratton, ME)
149	Stratton Brook Pond Rd.	9.1*	Stratton Motel (Stratton, ME)
150	Bog Brook Rd.	16.1*	Stratton Motel (Stratton, ME)
151	Pierce Pond Camps	16.5*	Hostel (Cabin)
152	Pleasant Pond Rd.	8.8*	Sterling Inn (Caratunk)
153	Moxie Bald Mt. Lean-to	13.6	Shelter
154	ME 15, Monson	17.9	Motel (Greenville)
155	Moosehead Lakefront Motel	0.0	Motel (Greenville)
156	Otter Pond parking	15.3*	Motel (Greenville)
157	Off Katahdin Ironworks Rd.	15.0*	B & B (Milo)
158	Logan Brook Lean-to	12.8	Shelter
159	Off Jo-Mary Rd.	15.4	Katahdin Inn (Millinocket)
160	Unnamed logging road	15.0*	Katahdin Inn (Millinocket)
161	Pollywog Stream parking	8.7 *	Katahdin Inn (Millinocket)
162	Golden Rd. Abol Bridge	17.2*	Katahdin Inn (Millinocket)
163	Katahdin Stream Campground	10.0*	Katahdin Inn (Millinocket)
164	Katahdin Summit	5.1*	Hilton Garden Inn (Bangor)

*Slackpack Day (Carrying only the bare minimum, including food for the day and water). All of the other days I carried a full pack. Although I wasn't carrying a tent, my full pack usually weighed between 24 and 28 pounds, depending on the amount of food and water I was carrying.

Even though I slept in a bed or bunk 145 of the 164 days of my hike, I only slackpacked 77 days.

I took 18 days off. Four of those were due to injury in Daleville, VA.

**Partial Slackpack Day

About the Author

MIKE STEPHENS IS A RETIRED English teacher and cross-country coach who lives in Columbus, Georgia. His first book, *Don's Brother: A Hike of Hope on the Appalachian Trail*, chronicles his 2,185.9 mile northbound thru-hike of the Appalachian Trail in 2013. The hike and the book were inspired by his brother, Don Stephens, who died of ALS (Lou Gehrig's disease) in August, 2012. Also an avid runner for over thirty-five years, Mike has completed forty-two marathons, including the Boston Marathon eight times. *The Don's Brother Method* is his second book.

Made in the USA
Middletown, DE
29 July 2023